MW00411709

REVERENCE *for* EXISTENCE

REVERENCE *for* EXISTENCE

A WAY OF KNOWING

CRAIG BRESTRUP

Camino Bay Books
Gualala, CA 95445

Copyright © 2018 by Craig Brestrup
All rights reserved. No part of this book may be reproduced or
transmitted in any form or by any means, electronic or mechan-
ical, including photocopying, recording, or by any information
storage and retrieval system, or internet program or system,
without written permission from the author.

Book design and publishing services: Constance King Design

Camino Bay Books
Box 9
Gualala, CA 95445
info@caminobaybooks.com
800-463-8181
ISBN: 978-0-9657285-0-8
Printed in USA

For wife Lynn and friend Ed—
Two who know

CONTENTS

I: Opening

— CHAPTER 1 —

THE SETTING

I WAS CAMPED IN THE eastern Sierra Nevada of California at 9,000' within a roughly enfolded basin, granite cliffs rising at least another 1,000' all around except for the gap through which the old glacier had eased downward fifteen millennia ago. A hiker approached to talk and share his feeling for the place. I listened quietly and without thinking responded that being in places like this makes us better people. I had surprised myself but knew it was true, just not how or from where the words came. In what ways do places like this make us better?

I have felt certain for many years about the connection between Nature's power and beauty and human moral and spiritual excellence, and there are others who share the conviction. In her study of Plato, American philosopher and author Rebecca Goldstein notes his "[...] view of the normativity of reality—that is, that we are morally improved by knowing what is what [...]" Plato was no "Nature writer," and meant something slightly different than what I experienced in the mountains that day, but not much. Cosmos manifests as truth-beauty-goodness, he believed—as intelligible order, and we are drawn to *know*. As we experience this—as we discern truth, feel goodness, behold beauty—the fitting reaction arises as love and surrender, or so I interpret. Self-forgetting for a time and then returning to self, turned away from what is lesser and unworthy within. We identify with what is greater: Cosmos, its delineated exemplifications and hovering ultimates, its wholeness. The world I work, play, hike, and live in every moment.

This is a lot to take in. At times, I am knocked over by the realization and feel full with love and knowing, but only at moments. Seven decades of living have left me with innumerable distortions, habitual ways, and defenses, and as such I am a poor representative of the inspired transformation of Plato's wise ones, whom he knew to be few. Coming up short defines the human condition as well as anything we can say about it.

To move toward realization, I honor reality as a first movement. Cosmic matter-energy took unfathomable beginnings and patiently fashioned, over unimaginable time and against the odds, a meadow in bloom and creatures to enjoy it. Since I stood in that glacier-carved basin ten years ago, during whatever I might be engaged in as time passed, the experience stayed with me: This is a finely made world that offers everything I need; the more I look the more I see and the more I want to look further and understand; satisfaction, completeness, en-lightenment...I just need to look. I say love that, then do what you will (taking liberty with St. Augustine's declara-tion). Goodness irresistibly follows, or would but for our many human deficiencies.

Aristotle described the flourishing life as one that was drawn toward and that amply embodied the dis-tinctive human excellences, the ethical and intellectual virtues. I would venture to add others such as the ex-cellence of an artist, craftsman, and other professional, people dedicated to distinctive traditions and practices and the goods for which they exist. I want to show throughout these pages that what I call reverence, and what others speak of in different but comparable ways, is both good for the soul and good for the world as it gives it what's due owing to its intrinsic nature. Reverence reveals value and fosters caring devotion where needed. And it begins with perceptive attention—with discovering ways to move through and beyond our limitations toward reverent existence.

Say you are outside, and you feel yourself moved by a starry night, a grand waterfall, a sunrise. A little surprised at the intensity, you take it seriously. It means something in addition to what's visible; it speaks to you in a language that you can recognize though you may not have a name for it. What's there? Something of mystery, but a sense that it coheres and is right. For a moment you listen, respond inwardly, and reflect upon it. Then you move on.

These are decisive moments. How seriously ought you to take them? You could turn away, return your attention to whatever preoccupied you before, rack it up as something pleasant, but no more than that.

But suppose you stay with it? You've sensed this before but can't quite recall...you remain open. Later, a piece of music nudges you back and the sensations and feelings return. You want better understanding so you revisit such places, pay attention, and begin to yield.

As you go along your normal ways, discrepancies between ordinary and extraordinary appear (they've always been there, but now you pay more attention). You seek ways to deepen experience. Still uncertain as to the meaning, you may stay with it in all seriousness.

Some people are drawn irresistibly to truth, "the truth of real things" (to borrow a phrase from Aquinas I've always thought apt). Truth about the realities of the physical world, the social and political worlds, the ethical world that suffuses the others.

I think of similar occasions for apprehension. While out hiking, I walk until a place speaks to me, and then I sit, look, and listen. I walk until another place speaks, and sit. Walk, sit. Horizontal being (quotidian reality) opens vertical (larger reality); vertical illuminates horizontal. Truth found in both. We discover both dimensions in different experiences. I was once a psychotherapist and worked with the same principle. My clients discoursed at will, and at moments we stopped, dug down, and reflected upon what we found. More discourse, stop, dig, reflect. It's a practice that combines everyday doing and being with attentiveness to the dimensions nested within ourselves and outer reality.

This practice leads to different ways of being: less haste and noise, more attentive. Each of those worlds— physical, social, political, ethical—benefits from this way of approaching and apprehending them.

The more seriously I take the wider and deeper world, the less seriously I take my narrow one of egoistic desire. I notice the animals, how they know who and where they are and exactly what their place here is. They are happy to live as the creatures they are. As gravity guides water along its way, the animals' fit to place and their animal consciousness tells them how to live most fully. Natural beings linked in ecological wholes manifesting the goodness of existence. My sensoria know and my moral and truth-seeking self knows, too: I can live in harmony.

Can we be as good as this world that birthed and sustains us? Can we deserve what it is and what it offers? What do we owe the world in return? Can we live so that we show it the respect it deserves and the gratitude it's due? I choose to tell these stories because I believe in the importance of the reciprocity implicit in what they reveal (and because I recognize so much failure on the human side of this partnership): the goodness we receive deserves an equal return in the form of protecting and sustaining that goodness, sometimes going so far as to pursue the restoration of damaged or lost goodness.

The word that works best for what I describe is *reverence.* The experience feels like a combination of the sense of holiness ordinarily implied by that word (toward a *mysterium tremendum,* in Rudolph Otto's term) and something less ethereal—the way we are sometimes moved in the deepest way, and usually to our surprise, by contact with something outside and greater than ourselves, but at the same time something that seems to embrace us. Nature, music, art, love...nontheistic piety, a response of profound veneration and connection with being.

Why believe there is anything more to this than an irrational spasm, gullible yearning, or emotional vapors? Its reality may feel self-evident as experienced but one's private knowledge, engendered in personal and virtually ineffable encounters with any of those *real things* that engage our deepest attention, reveals nothing credible to another who is unreceptive, who hasn't had such experiences, or who rejected them when she did.

I remember a philosopher, Robert Nozick, some years ago playfully exploring the question of how one could believe in God (which he did not). How would God signal his existence so that the receptive person would be justified in her faith? These are some of the characteristics he felt such a signal would have: it would be powerful and unambiguous as revelation of the divine, not dependent on particular forms of reasoning or language. It would be both symbol and analogue of Godly properties and as such command respect. Compellingly attractive, but in its essence unapproachable, unknowable. Enduring, impossible to miss; spectacularly beautiful, brilliant, dominant. And so on. He was describing the sun.

He pressed on to consider the role and meaning of faith: "[...] an encounter with something very real—an actual person, a person in a story, a part of nature, a book or work of art, a part of one's being—and this thing has extraordinary qualities that intimate the divine by being forms of qualities that the divine itself would have: these extraordinary qualities touch you deeply, opening your heart so that you feel in contact with a special manifestation of the divine, in that it has some form of divine qualities to a very great extent." Faith leads to belief, which relies on trust—trust that such deep responses cannot be doubted without fundamentally doubting oneself and one's perceptions.

I accept the reverence that certain encounters evoke as self-validating and sustained by trust. Whether a God has anything to do with them is beyond my comprehension. I doubt the existence of God as depicted by most believers, but as another word for the subject of those strangely profound responses of uplift, unity, wonder, and beauty that lead to reverence, I won't argue. I embrace these experiences as the most vital I have and take them to be telling me something. About what is and what ought. Truth and value.

In order to be more concrete about how this has been for me, I will tell a story, or rather a series of stories. Some of this book was written thirty years ago, but what you will find still illustrates as well as I can the experience of reverence as I have known it, from perception to reflection to revelation. I acknowledge that Nature is my own richest place of such encounters but do not want to imply that it is the only source. There are more facets to the jewel of revered existence than anyone can know—the bare fact of existence, in itself, unadorned, occasions reverence and from that beginning we may discover paths and ways to follow leading to more. I intend that this book serve as one signpost toward such paths and offer it in the humble hope that others will be encouraged to find their own.

— CHAPTER 2 —

CREATURES OF
BIG HART CANYON

IT ALWAYS SURPRISES ME — the canyon opens subtly at the edge of a meadow, descends gradually, and then plunges, all within shouting range of its inception. For this visit, I will be camped in a clearing on its eastern ridge two days before I venture in, anticipating its changes, its displays and revelations, and renewing my appreciation of other features of this favored place. I have been away too long.

A quarter-mile square, forty acres of southern Sierra Nevada wilderness in the Piute Mountains, the land is remote and mostly undisturbed. Two years ago, it became mine. It lies a tortuous hour's drive—ten miles—from the nearest full-time neighbor at the end of a meager, single-lane pathway that has long forgotten its last encounter with a maintainer blade. Only scant signs of predecessors remain.

I first saw it in spring, vibrant with wildflowers and quivering, eye-high agave seed stalks. The land is richly textured with granite that has been colorfully splashed with lichen and pinked from its primal subterranean brewing. Thick with juniper and mixed species of pine and oak, it rests at 5,500 feet with a ridge north at 7,000 and a valley below at 3,500. A transition zone, diverse and dry.

My attachment was first aroused by Big Hart Canyon, bisector and definitive feature of this ground. Born below a spring in the meadow immediately to the north, it begins as a modestly swelling arroyo. Then it grows bolder with a granite monolith guiding the water around itself and into the shadows beyond—a dramatic touch reminiscent of ranches that announce themselves with muscular gateways, but natural and unpretentious in this setting. Live oak and rill descend through a jumble of rock, cascades, fallen trees, tall grass and flowers. I clambered its length twice that first day, then spiraled around it up to a point where I could see the whole canyon embedded, enfolded as a crease within a wandering landscape. In semiarid country the little waterway inside its narrow and deepening crevasse stands out; it makes a distinctive biome, a creative expression of granite and gravity, geological patience coupled with biological exuberance. It entranced me.

Today I enter from the meadow and am soon halted abruptly just below the first waterfall. Certain sounds vibrate with authority and in this country a sibilant rattle rivets my attention. I have been moving down the canyon slowly in order fully to appreciate it and out of concern for the uncertain footing. Annie, fifty pounds of canine enthusiasm, moves ahead less prudently. As she bounds over a ledge, I hear simultaneously the thump of her landing and a vigorous maraca greeting. She has dropped into a snake's coiled midst. Momentum carried her beyond, curiosity drew her back, "ANNIE COME!" impelled her to me. We eased into an upward arc where we could safely look down upon the angry, thickset, and probably mortified rattlesnake. He buzzed resoundingly and fearsomely, but the great jaws were fully occupied with the hindmost end of a half-ingested rodent. He seemed vulnerable, and I wondered if discreet silence might have been better advised. (Or is rattling just what he does at these moments, caution be damned?) The threatening rasp went on; he stared fear and warning but neither struck nor swallowed: a snake's version of being caught with his pants down.

I walk on even more slowly. There are fewer flowers this dry year, but tree shade, rock shadow, and a secure feeling of earthy enclosure remain. A little farther and Big Hart's heart, the old canyon's dramatic center, unfolds. The V shape opens to a U. I work my way down to a smoothed rock surface about thirty yards long and half that wide with trees on the east slope, bouldered wall on the west, and a vast, falling vista to the south over the rock parapet. The abyss is ahead and to my right; a slick granite chute descends steeply for two hundred feet. The stream that found and deepened a crease in the granite behind does it here, too, undulating downward. It drops into a shallow basin near the bottom, then rolls out and down a short expanse, pools again, pauses, and finally disappears south. Big Hart Canyon graces other lands beyond mine, but differently: a more restrained drop and less green shade, but still impressive. I slip through the westside rock and cautiously make my way down to the little pool.

When land changes shape and cover as this does, there are always new ways to wander. After some time gazing up and around from the pool, I head west. Using hands and feet I ascend the steep canyon wall, find an animal trail, and return to camp through the meadow.

This meadow has particular appeal, something like an indeterminate promise. An expanse of thirty or so acres, encircled by oak and pine, a few great ponderosas scattered within, it is veined by the main spring flow and one or two ephemeral subsidiaries. It slithers southeast to my place. I learned something there the first morning we camped here over a year ago: a live oak with black bear cub scuttling up it in fear and mother bear launched from under in protective fury is never again just a tree. It amplifies to oak-bear sanctum, a place to pause quietly on approach. I have come to it most respectfully ever since that dawn encounter.

Up early that first morning, I grabbed coffee and meandered, led by Annie and our second dog, Mara. As we approached what was still only a tree, a sprawling old live oak with branches arching to the ground, the dogs dashed under, thinking they had found a chaseable creature. The cub ascended, seeking refuge from their assault and, predictably, his mother took offense. My recognition of the tree's transformation began with Annie and Mara's frantic emergence from beneath it, beelining for me with the mother in chase. She stopped and turned back toward the cub. Annie, rarely aggressive but always ebullient, halted and headed back after her, not yet understanding that this was not play. Mara, a Lab crippled by hip dysplasia only partially corrected by surgery, normally moves like a slow breeze through dense forest, but unlike Annie she fully understood the mistake they had made and did not hesitate in her labored course back, her movement more lively than usual. The mother turned to pursue Annie, who finally realized her misinterpretation and shot past me in the direction of camp.

Still rooted paralytically where I was when this began, I see Mara five yards in front of me, mother bear five yards behind her, every creature around except the cub and me in frenzied motion. As Mara heaved by, the bear halted, we looked inquiringly at each other, and then she turned back to her cub. Regaining breath and mobility, I turned and fell flat over a sagebrush. In a few minutes, we heard mother calling youngster down from the tree. When we come camping now the dogs always lie facing north toward that spot, lest she be there and remember.

Oak-bear place. On another visit, staked out with camera, we saw a lone bear cross the meadow toward the spring. Today when I pass through a brawny hawk calls and flies up to watch me from the top of a ponderosa. This meadow has a mysterious feel to it, and the spirit and power of these animals compose that in great part.

For millennia people have believed, and I am among them, that countless species have existed through numberless years and still do now in plenitude and beauty because life's creative spirit requires this abundance to express itself adequately. Creation is *one*, speaking with diverse voices. Without bear and hawk the meadow would be subdued, diminished. Yet by choice industrial-era humans do daily violence to beings by the millions, with needless, often merely careless, killing and habitat degradation, precipitating a sixth great extinction. A depth of suffering and loss hard to fathom, brought by our errant notions of the good for humans.

As I write these words it occurs to me that in large part this matter of the "good for humans," and how we conceive of and pursue it, may be key to the reciprocity I spoke of above between receiving and responding to the goods of existence, those things that allow value and meaning. For a long time, we appear to have confused material and technological progress with real human progress, a progress that would make for better societies, better human relationships, more love of truth and emotional and spiritual depth. Such misdirection from original goodness reminds me of Joni Mitchell's song from the '70s that spoke of "paving over paradise." We can only adequately respond to the gifts we receive when we differentiate real gifts from distractions. Without that, we mint our life's currency from "fool's gold." Stopping to remember both the thrill of danger and of wonder that now inhabits oak-bear place for me (and perhaps, also, for the dogs) brings these things into sharper focus.

This visit is my first in several months. I tried to get here twice during the winter but found it snowed in. Then I moved 1,200 miles north. As I drove south this trip and realized experientially the distance between new home and land, I thought of selling it: too expensive, too infrequent, too far. But I will not: too resonant, too much Hart and soul to relinquish. I knew it within an hour of arrival three days ago. It galvanized my senses and drew waves of emotion from my gut that turned into gratitude's tears.

Except for Annie, I came alone and ironically have not seen so many couples since leading marriage preparation workshops years ago. First evening, out of the valley to the east, a pair of red-tailed hawks ascend, riding the air and floating circuitously. Then one plunges toward the other, startling me—mock aggression, it seemed, part of their airy ritual. They appear to touch gently and then separate and soar synchronously. They fly these graceful motions for several minutes as if dancing, then one wings north while the other keeps circling. Astonished, I mull in wonder.

Within moments, *whirr-r-r-r*—a pair of California Quail breeze in and alight on the path a few yards away. He assumes watchful pose on a rock, she eats obliviously. Eventually he joins her at the meal but remains vigilant throughout: peck, peck, look around, peck. Each evening around 6:00 they make this same entrance, follow these same protocols. She is plump. He is sleek and protective.

I watch a pair of western tanagers as they flit about and watch me from the pines. Gaudy in their black, red, and yellow, but so timid that subdued colors would seem better suited to their personalities. Who knows what value their flamboyance has for them? Last evening I was fortunate to look up from my book just as they quietly barreled over. Playing and courting, twice joining, parting: another dance. Affection exchanged, perhaps love.

To my delight the show continues. A pair of western bluebirds arrive, take turns hovering curiously above me, then depart. Finches and warblers, scrub jays and rufous-sided towhees, a few unidentifieds. I feel as though camped within an avian love song. Their devotion inspires me. At home I have seen cardinal couples up to their knees in a feeder, when gently the male offers seed from his beak to hers. Why does he do that? Why hawks and tanagers dancing? Why ask? Are they so utterly different from us? Awe at the pleasing, perplexing rightness of such natural things just gives them their due.

Annie ends my reverie with a burst of foul breath as she returns from her rounds. The day before yesterday, which began with the bang of rattlesnake encounter, ended with a whimper still odorously echoed. I was watching birds at dusk and looked up the path to see

Annie in her stalking pose. Typically, this precedes a fu-
tile assault upon squirrels. She leaned over the path's
edge glaring, still as sculpture. I could not see her intended prey. She launched, but atypically boomer-
anged immediately, foaming at the mouth and wanting
my assistance. She plowed the ground with her snout,
dug frantically for looser dirt, circled, plowed, tunneled
through a pile of pine straw, then dug some more. She
had absorbed a direct hit to the mouth. A silent skunk
has resounding effects on a dog's composure and
breath. Twice during the night, she arose to vomit. Now
she is fine, except for her breath. I wonder if a rodent
grapevine spreads the news of justice rendered, and if it
also speaks of the snake and his victim?

The mountain north has a spot I like for its view and
setting and this time of year its wildflowers. As morning
clouds lift from its shoulders I fill my pack with water and
food, paper and pencil, and cross through the meadow.
The hawk cries warning as once again she lifts to the top
of a ponderosa, and I stand admiring through binoculars and trying to locate the nest I suppose she protects.
I cannot find it and have disturbed her enough; I head
northwest up the steep mountainside.

Climbing to the ridge I follow a trail up through
meadows separated by bands of granite outcropping
interspersed with trees and eventually arrive almost
due north of camp, 1,200 feet higher and perhaps a mile
away on line of sight. A tremendous view south into the
Tehachapi Mountains with their persistent haze. Much
of that is natural but I always suspect drifting infusion
of Central Valley pollution, a serious and disconcerting
matter. A steeply falling glade lies directly before me
decorated by lupine and assorted consorts. I write in

the shade of a live oak perfectly disposed for my purposes. Ground squirrels and birds *chirr,* sun shines,
breeze woos leaf and needle.

Four days here without sight of another human, yet
I have the distinct sense of companionship. Occasionally
eerie, it leads to reflection, alertness, a sense of appreciative connectedness. I can no more imagine flourishing without this immersion than without other humans.
Rooted in dirt and mystery, this natural world says most
of what I need to hear. Why not respond to such a voice?

I return by the meadow and notice signs that
free-ranging cows have been through. Since I quit eating them, I can think of but one quasi-positive thing
about these animals. Occasionally, when I bushwhack
through dense brush or over unstable footing, I intersect one of their trails and the going gets easier. But I
would trade that in an instant for their disappearance
from here. They shit prodigiously, trample the earth,
foul the spring, crush wildflowers, and chomp off the
agave's seed stalk—unforgivable since each plant has
but one progenitive opportunity then dies like a salm-
on before spawning. Except maybe, as I think about it,
for those piles of poop with their seedy cargo. What a
strange law that makes it my responsibility rather than
the cattleman's to keep them away.

Withal, they deserve pity and liberation from their
fate. Part Nature and part artifact, lives nasty, brutish,
and short, climaxed in slaughter. (Here on this mountain maybe not so nasty and brutish but still short and
with the same terminus.) Like all domesticated animals, they are diminished versions of their ancient ancestors. We treat them shamelessly, as if mere objects,
and show a decent respect neither for them nor the

land and indigenous creatures hurt by their presence.

Contemporary treatment of farmed, or "food," animals illustrates vividly a case of lost reverence. All these animals are descendants of wild forebears, animals who were shaped by evolution to flourish in certain habitats and ecosystems alongside other wild animals with the same purpose. For efficiency and profit, convenience and taste, we have altered them beyond recognition and imposed empty and often painful lives. Surprisingly, though, even these diminished and distorted beings, when you open to them, look into their eyes and see inexpungable individuality and sentience...even they look back and remind us that they make a claim for respect just as we do. Our innate, too often shirked, responsibility and a sort of joy appear when we honor that claim.

Days pass, time shortens; I must leave. This last morning, I rise to a heavy dew, so wet it could almost have showered. Fog drifts in and rolls out. I start a fire to warm and illuminate as only campfires can. Later I walk down into the side of the canyon.

Though I usually feel well acquainted with this land and all its aspects, random walks reveal new perspectives and visions. This time I find a mystic garden spot below the first waterfall, above the snake's ledge on the east side. I hear without seeing the water and look across through trees toward gleaming efflorescence. Even Annie stills, as if moved in uncommon ways for her. But time will not slow. We walk. An acorn woodpecker, the first I have seen, alights on a pine snag and searches. On into the meadow, the hawk silent, maybe aware she has outlasted me.

I pack and leave slowly, taking an hour and a half to drive the eighteen miles down out of this range into the desert. As I drive, I think of the meadow and its oak-bear grove and recollect my "bearanoid" hikes in Alaska. What is a right relation between humans and non-humans? What do we gain and what do we lose living predominantly in a constructed world, designed and subdued for our pleasure and convenience? I am convinced by the meadow and canyon that they can help me fathom the world's mysterious otherness and inherent meanings and values simply by existing in their own excellent ways as they do. Sharing Earth, I identify with the animals, plants, landscapes—all those others with whom I share existence in this place.

The animals' presence wove this visit whole. I wanted solitude, and except for airplanes and noise of a chainsaw one day in the distance, I have had no awareness of other people, but I never felt alone. I fear the snake's venom and the bear's strength, but both land and experience would be impoverished without their powerful presence. Hawk, skunk, even Annie: each is part of the fullness.

A few days before I left for here, as I arrived at work, I was drawn to a pond where violet green swallows swept the air for breakfast. I had not known them before. My first evening on the mountain I sip wine and recover from the miles, then realize I am haloed by violet green flight. It seemed a greeting and a linking—another revelation of Earth wonder.

Note: After this visit, out of respect for the other animals, I kept Annie on a leash as I always should have. She doesn't mind the restriction, but the others whose home it is minded her freedom.

— CHAPTER 3 —

OCCASIONS

Gifts

SOMETIMES A SENSATION OVERCOMES ME intense to the point of tears, but it is more often a background presence that tells me I am among other creatures who profoundly matter—human and not human, plant and animal, venerated others. This sense of things is what I mean by reverence, which seems to me the most fitting response to the natural world and to existence as a whole and its varied manifestations.

Robin Kimmerer is a botanist who has managed to integrate scientific knowledge and methodologies with a Native American perspective that matches in many ways what I describe. She enters the forest:

> I come here to listen, to nestle in the curve of the roots in a soft hollow of pine needles, to lean my bones against the column of white pine, to turn off the voice in my head until I can hear the voices out-side it: the *shhh* of wind in needles, water trickling over a rock, nuthatch tapping, chipmunks digging, beechnut falling, mosquito in my ear, and something more—something that is not me, for which we have no language, the wordless being of others in which we are never alone.

She knows there is a language of the woods, knows too that science speaks only a few of its words and that there is more she can learn. She calls it a "grammar of animacy" and her responses respect the speaking and the source. One example, which her grammar shares with that of believers in the inherent value of animals (animal rights people), shuns speaking of them as "it." They are he's and she's and those who fly over. Gestures of respect along with Sir and Ma'am toward our elders.

Reverence and virtue (in the ancient sense) are one, each fully infused with the other. Virtues are ways of excellence, ethically and intellectually, practices aimed at goodness and truth. Their engagement is how reverence gets down to work. Irreverence, in this case, does its business very differently. Mountain-top-removal mining, clear-cut forestry, chemicalized industrial agriculture, and factory farming of animals all come to mind. These practices strike me as being as far from goodness as they could possibly be and ignorant and uncaring about both their near and long term effects and their cruelty.

Alternatively, Kimmerer speaks of the Honorable Harvest, "[...] the indigenous canon of principles and practices that govern the exchange of life for life [...] rules of sorts that govern our taking, shape our relationships with the natural world, and rein in our tendency to consume [...]" Small ways, large ways; apparent or not, reverence makes the world and the doer and the doing better. Touch with care, take in moderation, feel a reflexive gratitude: these are the gifts that enrich existence.

What does it mean to experience life as an array of gifts? Is it analogous to Christian "grace," which recognizes that people don't earn or even necessarily deserve their God's compassion; rather, through His grace-filled, grace-defined gifts they may grow more godlike in mercy and love? To begin with a strong sense that cosmic origin, development, formations (Earth, life, consciousness), evolutions, transitions, all that we have and all that led to this particular here and now—to begin in certainty that all this was in the nature of a *gift* infuses perception and experience with added dimension. Years ago, when I stopped taking existence for granted and gave up the idle notion that everything that is and has been was centered on *Homo sapiens,* nothing looked quite the same as before. Everything looked more unique, more valuable.

To receive a gift invites gratitude and reciprocity. Giftedness is a relational link between giver and receiver. *Being* itself is the original gift and great giver. Look at all that it offers. One can wake from his or her ordinary strivings, as if the light that follows some storms or sunrises suddenly shone and continues shining, and things are new.

The light too is a gift. Lewis Hyde's fine book, *The Gift,* speaks of the gifts of artistic creation:

> That art that matters to us—which moves the heart, or revives the soul, or delights the senses, or offers courage for living, however we choose to describe the experience—that work is received by us as a gift is received [...] The spirit of an artist's gifts can wake our own. The work appeals, as Joseph Conrad says, to a part of our being which is itself a gift and not an acquisition. Our sense of harmony can hear the harmonies that Mozart heard. We may not have the power to profess our gifts as the artist does, and yet we come to recognize, and in a sense to receive, the endowments of our being through the agency of his creation. We feel fortunate, even redeemed. The

daily commerce of our lives [...] proceeds at its own constant level, but a gift revives the soul. When we are moved by art we are grateful that the artist lived, grateful that he labored in the service of his gifts.

Saying yes to art, yes to Nature, yes to all the gifts—this is a way that has the potential to change everything. Or, rather, it doesn't change anything—"the daily commerce of our lives [...] proceeds at its own constant level"—except our way of experiencing the days we are given and how they can best and most fittingly be used. *Everything becomes more interesting, more alive:* walk in the forest or even a city street and see for yourself.

And this way of moving through life compels us even farther: It leads us to want more of the same. When we experience beauty, for example, it evokes veneration, joy, and the desire to protect and replicate it. Beauty arouses a sense of sacredness, love, of indubitable rightness, goodness, of wishing to stay in its presence. This is what leads me to reverence time and again. Having arisen in and from Nature, feeling myself a particle shed from its body, recognizing how it sustains all that I value, immersed in awe—what else would I feel? What greater gift is there?

I think that this gift of reverence is one of the salient features of shared moral and physical landscapes. You feel entwined, identified with other givers and receivers of gifts. Solidarity with the forest, with Nature, defines the relationship between self and world. With nonhuman animals, humans, communities: relations become respectful and compassionate. Why wouldn't they? All share the gift, all are within the oneness and each may sometime need my active care and I theirs. The way of reverence is more interesting, more complex, deeper and more satisfying. It's the way of fewer commodities, yet more gifts.

Love

Once, I was camped in the Sierra Nevada a couple of hundred miles north of where I was at the beginning of these pages. On that day, I hiked in the morning, returned to camp for lunch, read for a couple of hours, and then lay down for a short nap. I didn't sleep deeply but seem to have fallen into a state of immense calm somewhere between sleep and wakefulness.

From the unconscious came a sensory imagining, a vivid dream, clear and real. I was quite old, evidently dying, and in a hospital—a place toward which I have the strongest aversion. My wife Lynn entered the room and, sharing my aversion, was glad to help when I said I must leave and go home. No one tried to stop us and I next found myself in our courtyard, sitting in my favorite spot under a giant elm filling my senses with the beauty of the place. Behind us, the elm and me, south of the house, is a bluff sixty to seventy vertical feet with a steep slope covered in smaller trees, mostly juniper and hackberrry, along with shrubs and rock. Deer and chickens are often seen browsing there. Within the courtyard are more trees and a wide selection of flowering plants that Lynn has introduced and cared for. Our home is a half mile from the narrow county road and without neighbors, so there are rarely any but natural sounds.

As I sat there alone in the shade, knowing that death was imminent, I was unexpectedly overcome with the splendor, the immensity, of it all, more deeply moved than I may ever have been, filled with a love that some might call agape; a spiritual love lacking self-interest-edness, a thing in itself that happened to use my consciousness as a momentary medium for entering the world of awareness. I was more than filled; I was taken over by it, suffused with love and gratitude. It seemed that my knowledge of dying and my incarnating this love were fully present to each other and harmonious. There was poignancy but not sadness that I would soon lose Nature—or rather lose consciousness of Nature as I died and returned my body to its further uses—but I felt grateful for having been given life, no regrets or protests at leaving. I was immersed in love and that was all and enough.

It lasted only a few moments. Lying there in camp, I returned to everyday consciousness, but stunned at what I had experienced. I wanted to go back to that love and that place but could not. The mystics say that mere humans are not able to find ecstasy except briefly, and so this was, whatever it was. I got up and walked through the great pines among which I was camped, everything but the memory normal again.

I have read accounts from two monks and a scientist who suffered strokes. Each marveled at the access to love that was opened by the impairment, permanently for the monks. Bede Griffiths, for example, a Benedictine/Hindu monk who died in India in 1993: Shirley du Boulay, his biographer, said that "[...] what was remarkable about Bede's last days was that at last he was free of any remaining vestiges of the repression that had dogged his life; he had reached his full humanity [...] his capacity for love and affection, already liberated by his first stroke and the experience which accompanied it, found expression as never before."

I wonder if my experience of dying served similarly, if its extremity opened me to what is always there beneath consciousness. I have felt a vital, abiding love for Nature for over thirty years with occasional upsurges sparked by certain settings or landscapes, enraptured moments of powerful emotion and realization. But none was quite like this one, which even days later remained a glow on my inner horizons.

I ask what the experience has to teach me. I ask also why, with such depth and intensity, such realness, this revelation of love, apparently subsisting within, is so shy. Or maybe the responsibility is mine, my limitations. Still, it seems right as it is, a vision of beatitude, a sign, a gift, a recollection. Love is at the heart of things, it says, essence of spirit, the mysterious wholeness and *is-ness* that unites the multiplicities of existence. I cannot understand or describe it; a sense, an intuition, experiences like this confirm. I think it impossible to peer into such realms, to be moved in such ways, and not feel reverence for existence. I know nothing of a creator God or of supernal realms removed from this one. This world is enough, and I honor it for occasionally lifting its veil.

Human Nature

I have previously mentioned Rebecca Goldstein's discussion of Plato and the implication she drew about the "normativity of reality." The background for this was Plato's belief that some people have a deep innate drive to know the truth. The words she imaginatively put in his mouth were these: "Perhaps the best name for it is love of wisdom [...] Those who have this trait love the truth not because it is like this or like that. They love the truth simply because it *is* the truth and are prepared to love it no matter what it turns out to be." (These days we are so aware of the universal danger of confirmation bias and motivated reasoning, not to mention "alternative facts," exemplified preeminently in ideological hardening of the mental arteries, that such a drive for the truth is almost beyond imagining.) Normative reality points toward a close association of facts and values: truth as both factual and ethically laden.

Plato linked the love of wisdom with that of beauty (while fearing that beauty could overcome wisdom in certain souls), and as that love moves us out of ourselves, beyond ego, he thought we are equally drawn toward goodness—to love and to act for moral and ethical good. The drive toward these ultimates is involved with human nature, and I use that bland word "involved" deliberately for I cannot know how deep or universal the involvement is. Only that some people are captured by it. And it may be that for all people it is crucial to their having "a life worth living." A less ominously judgmental way of putting that would be as crucial to their having a worthy life, the kind of life that you would recommend to others as exemplary for its honor and meaningfulness, its value to the world as well as the person.

A very similar way of viewing things was ascribed to Martin Buber, the late Jewish philosophical anthropologist, who of all the influences on my thinking goes back the farthest and has endured for close to fifty years. He was described by one commentator as striving "to ethicize the human sphere altogether." Meaning that he believed the essence of human life was rooted in relationship, and that implicit in relationship is the demand for responsibility: you must respond to the other's address (what he or she asks of you, says to you, needs from you) and you are accountable for how you respond.

Both these ways, of Plato and Buber, imply something about human nature. They aren't preaching to us; they are describing how in fact they believe we are built and that the ways in which we recognize our nature and seek means and ends that fulfill it are determinative of the worthiness of our lives along with their satisfactions and meaning. The sense I had standing in the midst of that high mountain valley surrounded by those craggy granite peaks, the sense that being in that presence made me a better person, was not just an idiosyncratic, romanticized response. It revealed that there is something innate in us, in our nature, that can respond with awe to reality and that in allowing that response we become more of who we actually are and are improved by it (morally, spiritually, in our sensibilities). Buber goes so far as to say that we only fulfill ourselves, only become fully who we are, through the responsible mutuality of relationship.

Reverence begins in the bare awareness of being, of things existing, and of finding that wondrous, enchanted. After all, there might have been nothing at all, no existence, period. Or the something that did exist might never have moved beyond lifeless energy and matter (think about what's been called the "fine-tuned universe" and all those fundamental physical constants that had to have been as they are or reality would have been very different and without anything like Earth or us). Reverence then carries me to those places where the wonder is repeatedly brought back to awareness and personal change happens because we are built for that. Buber spoke of it as "Thou-relation," those times when we respond most deeply to another, any other: person, animal, Nature, work of art...and recognized these as the places where meaning is found, and love, and where we fulfill our nature.

— CHAPTER 4 —

ON THE NATCHEZ TRACE

Almost thirty years ago, I took a trip from Texas to South Carolina. As I reflect on this journey now, I think of it as unconsciously going in search of confirmation for the growing reverence I felt toward Nature. Here is how I described what happened along the way.

I DISCOVERED THE NATCHEZ TRACE PARKWAY fortuitously in 1988. I was to go from Texas to Charleston, South Carolina for two days consulting, had just gotten a pick-up truck and camper, and decided to take the week off and use the trip for a trial run in preparation for longer trips West in the fall. I allowed a leisurely three days to travel each way and in looking at the maps for a "blue highway" itinerary saw the Parkway. Knowing nothing more than that it went my direction for roughly a hundred miles, I decided to try it.

The Parkway is part of the National Park Service, an unusual part in that it encompasses 45,000 acres ribboning out over 408 miles (eventually 450) between Natchez, Mississippi and just south of Nashville, Tennessee. From the late eighteenth century into the early nineteenth, thirty to forty years in all, it was the route of roads and "traces" (barely visible paths through wilderness) which kept the then American Southwest in some degree of connection to its eastern centers. For centuries prior to that it had been a path for animals and Native Americans. In addition to natural beauty, the area carries a rich history.

Since my first encounter with the Trace, I have driven parts of it on three occasions but until now never its entire length in one trip. Its temporary beginning near Natchez is about eight miles north of its true origin. Coming from Natchez you enter the Trace after several miles of driving one of those corridors that have become typical of city perimeters: divided highway, fast food outlets, convenience stores, run-down auto parts dealers, and so on. When I entered it for the first time, with no fore-knowledge and little expectation, I was stunned. And captured. Its contrast with what preceded my arrival, its natural beauty and seeming isolation were stark, and I spent the next several hours driving, walking, and learning how rapt is the adjective for rapture.

I returned this time to further my connection with this unusual landscape. In the narrative, "Old Trace" refers to the original trail while "Trace" refers to the present corridor as a whole.

Nine Days on the Trace

From my home in East Texas to Natchez is 175 miles of forest, former (i.e., logged) forest, and farm land. I find the four hours' drive a time of sadness alternating with hope. No matter what else may be true, it is impossible to eradicate hope in the spring. Dogwood, wisteria (some climbing to the tops of great trees—splendid decoration but I imagine a burden for limbs that have other things to do), azaleas, and more wildflowers than I have name-remembering capacity. Their exuberant color reminds me that we owe much of the world's beauty to the aesthetic tastes of insects. Wonderful abundance.

But then there are clear-cuts. Of the many savage things humans do to the world, clear-cuts are for me one of the worst. For lumber and profits we trade ecological integrity and get back indiscriminate destruction and long years of ugliness. I can't stop feeling appalled. Mile after mile separated from the road only by "decorative" borders of uncut trees ten to thirty yards wide, it lays there decimated, suffering, a desert in the negative sense of that word, an arboreal Hiroshima. Are the ribbons of remaining forest a residual concern for highway aesthetics or only an effort to disguise what has been done? They should bring the bulldozers and cutting machines right up to the road and make us face our choices.

In Natchez, before heading for the Trace, I decide to visit the Grand Village of the Natchez Indians. Although the town and eventually the Trace were named for them, the Natchez Indians were eradicated as a discrete tribe in the early eighteenth century. The Natchez culture was centuries old and from 1682 until 1729 the Grand Village was the tribal center. An early French immigrant called them "one of the most polite and affable nations on the Mississippi." The Village is dominated (unless I look over my shoulder to the west at encroaching ranch-style brick homes) by two large mounds, one for the former home of the "Sun" (chief) and the other the Temple Mound. When a Sun died the house atop his mound was burned and the mound raised a bit higher for his successor. Then his wife and retainers were ceremonially strangled and buried with him in the Temple Mound. Suns very likely had numerous people who earnestly wished them health and long life.

In 1716 the French built Fort Rosalie near the Grand Village and, as Europeans abroad were wont to do, proceeded to exploit the locals in whatever ways they could. In 1729, the Natchez learned that the French intended to expropriate more of their land (including the Grand Village) and decided they had had enough. They entered the fort under a ruse and killed several hundred, mutilating and decapitating as they went, and took a number of women captive. Shortly afterward the French, with Choctaw allies, retaliated, killing most, selling others into slavery, and dispersing the rest who eventually were assimilated into other tribes. So ended the Natchez culture.

Now I enter the Trace. The surprise left when familiarity arrived, but re-entry and recognition are intensely pleasurable. As alien as the road in was, being here conveys a strong sense of home-on-Earth. No commercial vehicles, no billboards or advertising, reduced speed limit, the only modern artifacts vehicles, roadway, and informational markers: a moving meditation. Two weeks ago, when I was here, the woods were winter gray betrayed only by buds and precocious dogwood. Leaf and blossom have now taken over.

The Trace covers three topographical zones. This section where I enter (and for about a hundred miles) is "Deep South": agricultural, swampy in places, cypress, magnolia, oak, pine, Spanish moss, summer heat. Over the Trace's course are said to be at least 100 species of trees, 215 of birds, 57 of mammals, and 89 of reptiles and amphibians—most of these native. Gone are buffalo, elk, wolf, cougar, black bear, passenger pigeon, Carolina parakeet, and ivory-billed woodpecker. As I go north I will climb into the second zone and then drop down into Tennessee, where cropland will more frequently intersperse with forest.

The first travelers here were animals, Native Americans, traders, soldiers, "Kain-tucks" (the generic name for boatmen, men who rode rafts full of goods down the Ohio, Tennessee, and Cumberland Rivers to the Mississippi and thence to Natchez or New Orleans to sell both boat and contents and walk back to homes in Tennessee, Ohio, Kentucky, and surrounding areas), postriders (Nashville to Natchez with the mail in under ten days if the rider survived), itinerant preachers, outlaws and settlers. After 1716, the French claimed dominion of this area, then in 1763 the British took over (and called the Old Trace "Path to the Choctaw Nation"), then Spain in 1779 ("Camino de Cumberland a Natches") and finally in 1798 the United States ("Natchez Trace"). As before, with the French and Natchez Indians, much of the tale is violent and blood-stained. Time and beauty heal, it appears.

Two miles into the Trace I come upon Emerald Mound. Built by ancestors of the Natchez Indians between 1300 and 1600 CE, it is about a mile from the road. If anyone knows what happened to these people, none among my sources seems to know. Although it may not be relevant to the Trace's history (except in early and unknown ways), I cannot resist sites like this so I spend some time walking around it and imagining. The "Great Platform" is flat and rectangular, about eight acres in all (770' x 435' x 35'), either the second or third largest in the United States; it probably had eleven smaller mounds on it originally although only a large one at the south end and a smaller one at the north remain. It was a religious and cultural center for local Native Americans. Probably a temple once sat atop the large remaining mound. To construct Emerald Mound the top of a hill was clipped off and that dirt, along with many an individually carried basketful from the area, were piled and packed together. Standing on it today, I look out on surrounding forest. Although thirty-five feet doesn't sound high, the view is impressive. Even these early Native Americans experienced the apparently ubiquitous need for sacramental earth modification, to raise up and set apart and so to set eyes looking up or down, to manipulate as well as adapt, to set a mood, an ambience, for ritual, worship, and ceremony. Important differences between them and us, but in some regards more technological than psychological.

A little farther and I arrive at Mount Locust, the only restored "stand" on the Trace. Built in 1870, Mount Locust, like most of the fifty eventual stands, started as a settler's home and evolved into a stand because of the traffic and the opportunity it afforded the settler to augment his income. Stands provided food, a place to sleep, safety, and occasionally provisions. This one, like several of the others, eventually became sufficiently well-equipped to graduate to the status of "inn."

I camp for several days at Rocky Springs, about fifty miles up the Trace and near the site of a town by that name of which only the Methodist Church, built in 1837, still stands. Adjoining it is the prototypical ancient cemetery: near-permanent shade from giant oaks and pines and Spanish moss, headstones broken and faded. A palpable solemnity hangs in the air. A few of the graves have enormously tall trees rooted directly where a body once lay.

The Powers, John R. and Sara V., had three infant children laid side-by-side between October 1851 and July 1853. Across the way another Powers child, Ella (one month old), lies under heartfelt verse:

> *As the sweet flower that scents the morn,*
> *But withers in the rising day.*
> *Thus lovely was this infant's dawn,*
> *Thus swiftly fled its life away.*

Harriet Naomi Hamer's family felt cheated by her death. Her stone says, "26 years, 4 months, 3 days":

> *I need not say how one by one,*
> *Affection's flowers have dropped*
> *from off affection's chain;*
> *Enough to say that they are gone,*
> *And that they cannot bloom again.*

I admire the personalization in these old cemeteries. Death was more familiar to these people and seems to have been more poignant. Since people stopped tending (and entering) family plots they have become anonymous and efficient. There must have been a certain satisfaction in knowing you would meet eternity in a place like this, even with (maybe because of) a tree eventually sprouting through your chest.

I visit one more before I go: A family plot that has a brick wall around it. About four feet high, two bricks thick (fourteen to fifteen inches), and eighteen feet square, it can only be entered through a narrow break in the wall over a twenty-inch high step. This fortress was built to last—over a century old and well intact.

Why did they do this? Was the family relatively isolated from the community in life? Did they seek to dissuade animals from treading on their graves? Pride? Fear? I leave wondering.

South of the church, a facsimile picture of what Rocky Springs probably looked like at its pre-Civil War height (population in 1860: 2,616) shows a pleasant place of homes and fields, streets and businesses. Merchants, physicians, teachers, artisans, and above all (the adjoining description emphasizes) planters and slaves lived here. A genuine photo, circa 1900, shows the church and a few structures barely holding on amongst shocking ravines and generally eroded, devastated land, the result of building an exploitative plantation culture and thought-less agricultural practices on, you might say, imported soil. Loess dust blew in during the last Ice Age covering the old clay and sand seabed with from thirty to ninety feet of loose dirt. It didn't weather well as the former Rocky Springs and those portions of the Old Trace called the "Sunken Trace" (ten to fifteen feet below the rim) tes-tify. Today old Rocky Springs, below the tough old church, is jungly ravine—lush verdance with no signs of human works beyond historical markers and snack wrappers.

Walking a few miles of the Old Trace nearby, I noticed at one stretch that I involuntarily stopped humming, softened and slowed my steps, mind quieted, breathing deepened: I'd come under a canopy of great old pine and hardwood (fifty to one hundred years old) generously draped with moss, filtered light, and silence.

This morning, 3:16 a.m., a cardinal called, a single seven-note series, then quiet, then return calls from owls and others, then silence. This happened several times during the night. What were they talking about?

After breakfast I walked the trail (itself barely a "trace" after a winter's disuse) to Owens Creek Falls—six miles out and back through old forest and hills, heavily ravined, occasionally almost swamp. The *feel* of the place almost overcomes me; lest I grow excessive and wearisome I will reserve comment on its beauty and stick to a few simple observations: in places it is thick with dogwoods which, even on this cloudy day, glow whitely through the understory; beech trees appeal to me, one reason being their proclivity toward opening cavities in their trunks near the ground yet growing on—I'm sure the creatures appreciate it as well, come storms; gnarled old, huge sycamore hanging tight on eroding bank of stream, knobby exposed roots with concavities in which small purple flowers rooted and bloomed; brown duff yields to green of forest floor covering; moss and fern proliferate; wild turkey flushed.

Owens Creek Falls turns out to be two small ones on creeks just before their confluence. Waterfalls have inexplicable powers to move me, even wee ones like these. In general, emotions seem to emerge from anywhere between the eyes and the navel. Those coming from below appear deepest, and from the navel less from grief than exaltation. There is where falls affect me. The present ones are modest—thin sheets of water only ten feet from lip to pool, eroded under grotto-like, the one I particularly admired making a quick oxbow turn to the south from pool, mossy-edged bowl surrounding, and all this at the base of steep, verdant hill. I can spend a long time at places like this.

On my way back I discover a small cemetery I had missed coming in, not surprisingly since it differed from the surrounding forest only by virtue of small fading headstones. Untended and forgotten, grown over as if not there. Presumably this was once an outlying homestead to Rocky Springs although there are no signs of former habitation other than the graves, the most recent of which is dated 1912, about the time of the town's demise. Only nine discernible graves and one of the most poignant cemeteries I have entered. Side-by-side were these three stones:

John Jackson Harper
Born June 15, 1838
Auburn, Macon County, Alabama
Died October 30, 1878
Rocky Springs, Claiborne County, Mississippi
1st Lieut. "Van Dom Guards," CSA
Son of Thomas H. and Elizabeth W. J. Taylor Harper.

Olive Branch Powers
Wife of John J. Harper
Born 1835
Claiborne County, Mississippi
Died August 21, 1878
Claiborne County, Mississippi
Daughter of Henry G. J. and Laura J. Hedrick Powers.

Willie W.
Son of John J. and Olive Branch Powers Harper
Born September 9, 1867
Died November 1, 1875
"Our Little Willie Sleeps Sweetly Here"

A nestled lamb tops Willie's headstone. A family came and went too quickly.

Then, two more, both topped with doves:

Allie H.
Daughter of J. M. and A. L. Flowers
Born November 30, 1885
Died June 6, 1887

Henry G.
Son of J. M. and A. L. Flowers
Born July 20, 1881
Died August 5, 1887

The summer of 1887 was a time of pain for the Flowers; maybe they moved on and away from it—they aren't buried here.

One more, a John J. Harper (1869-1899), perhaps another son of John Jackson and Olive Branch, has a hand on his marker with three fingers and thumb clenched, index finger pointing up. The origin of that curious symbolism lays with Reverend Zebulon Butler, Presbyterian minister in nearby Port Gibson from 1828 until he died in 1860. Said to have been a "power in the pulpit," the reverend commonly drove home his point with this hand gesture. Eventually a large wooden version, covered in gold leaf, was fashioned and mounted on the steeple. (On my return trip I divert to Port Gibson to see if it remains; it does—a replica—left hand high atop the steeple where a cross normally resides.)

More than a century has passed since these people lived and died here and this land was cottoned and eroded out. The forest has reclaimed its ground. As I leave, I notice the Trace roadway barely visible below and to the east a quarter mile.

I discovered on my return strange (to me) plants growing by my camp. Two large leaves, mostly seven-lobed, about six inches off the ground, each plant with a single white blossom falling from an inch-long stem emerging from the fork of the two leaves, thus practically hidden. Defense, understatement, unnecessary modesty? It's really rather a plain flower.

Fireflies swarmed around camp last night. This is the first time I have seen any in a long time (I had considered the possibility they might have been done in by insecticides) and this many at once, it's been a very long time. They hovered about my area casting meager, mysterious light for over an hour, when either they left or my attention wandered. Nothing evokes childhood like fireflies.

As I drive along the Trace, I realize that along with my appreciation for its continuous beauty I have a sense of it as a kind of allegory. As both park and roadway, something of the former is lost while the latter gains returns on that at a high rate of interest. Compare this with Yosemite Valley, for example, which is supposedly exclusively park while often seeming like a freeway at rush hour. The Trace represents humans placing limits on ourselves in terms of speed, commercial traffic and advertising, tree cutting, and efficiency (imagine only one convenience store for 408 miles) in return for unlimiting ourselves relative to historical awareness, recognition of how the land once was, and the chance to immerse in Nature's presence. Although devotees of untouched wilderness will find it not fully satisfying, as an example of touching with care and thought the Trace represents what we can do when we will.

Another aspect of its story is to reveal loss, apparent most strikingly whenever one enters or leaves the

Trace. Roadway aggression, careless and destructive impositions on the natural world, the trading of beauty and order for clashing mosaic of sensory dissonance— might it have been possible to make roadways and by-ways less efficient but kinder to sensibilities? Might we start with the land as it is and adapt our wants in some measure rather than unleashing boundless wants and demanding that land (and eventually we as well) adapt?

It is a curious thing to me that as parents we see the wisdom in instructing our children that they cannot have everything they want. We tell them that's not the way the world works and that, in any event, it is a fool's game to pursue it. And then, as the words leave our mouths and hang in the air about us, we turn around and proceed with the adult business of trying to have everything we want.

As I write it has now been some ten days since the Valdez oil spill turned Prince William Sound into an oily charnel house for wildlife, a symbol of human gluttony and shame. Here, once again, our unwillingness to limit our wants and means plays havoc with natural value. Haste for oil and profits by Congress and oil companies back in 1973 brought the oil to Valdez, where risks and vulnerabilities were high, rather than overland through Canada to join existing pipelines. Anger and grief are tempered only with unhappy resignation.

While my thoughts are turning sad and away from the Trace, I remember that just before I left on this trip I learned that Edward Abbey had died— "internal bleeding" was all I was told, mid-March it happened. He was in his early sixties—too early to end. Through his writing, I cared for him. In place of Joseph Wood Krutch's wise and elegant desert reflections, Abbey put passionate iconoclasm. He seemed of a piece with sand and canyon. Somewhere he wrote that when he died he wanted only to be laid out on desert sand and left for the buzzards. If that remained his wish at the end, I hope it was honored.

Thinking of desert, I recently learned the devious rationale behind the saguaro's "cuddling" behavior with palo verde and chaparral (something I noticed on a trip west). It seems he appreciates the shade, it helps him survive. Decades pass before he is as tall as his bene-factors and the shade lets the time pass more comfort-ably. And then, in a gesture of mammoth ingratitude, he wildly spreads his roots and starves his companions. What a world.

I notice as I drive north that the dogwood, wildflow-ers, and trees appear a week or so behind those at the beginning. Somewhere the change came on abruptly. I also notice that almost all the farms and houses that oc-casionally abut the Trace seem especially well tended, as if maybe proximity to this handsome corridor influ-enced farmers to keep up the good work. Urban sociol-ogists have long known that abandoned buildings take much longer for the first window to get smashed than for the second, and so on in decreasing units of time, as if even vandals have a certain responsiveness to things as they are. Perhaps farmers have a similar but opposite response to the Trace.

Yesterday I stopped in the area of Doak's Stand near the first "revised" Choctaw Boundary. At the turn of the nineteenth century the Choctaw Nation occupied roughly the lower sixty percent of what is today Mississippi. Their 20,000 people resided in sixty or seventy villages. The Chickasaw occupied the land north of them into today's Tennessee and probably were never more than 5,000 people. Although other Native Americans had lived in these areas for millennia, the Choctaw and Chickasaw mythology told that they had come from the west as a single group at a time no one could remember and subsequently, for reasons equally mysterious, had separated. R. S. Cotterill suggests it may have been due to Chickasaw contempt for Choctaw adoption of certain "heathenish" customs, e.g., wearing long hair, flattening their infants' heads by binding them to a board several hours a day, and picking the flesh from the bones of their dead. He also describes these and other of the southern tribes as managing to meld economic communism with individual liberty, a combination which largely freed them from ambition for either wealth or power.

Returning to the revised Choctaw boundary, the meeting between expansionist America and Native Americans in the early nineteenth century may have been the first conflict between communism and capitalism, and the latter decisively won. Following decades of competition among the French, Spanish, and British over and through Native American lands, the United States took dominion in 1798. Immediately, pressures to settle these lands grew and in 1820 the Treaty of Doak's Stand arranged an exchange of five and a half million Choctaw acres (one third of their total) for land west of the Mississippi and a few dollars to get started with. Few Choctaw were pleased with the arrangement since it would mean emigration, but they were given little choice. Ten years later the Treaty of Dancing Rabbit Creek took the remaining two thirds and the infamous "Indian removal" began. Similar processes and more treaties brought the Chickasaw to the same pass in 1832. Grant Foreman quotes a certain Chief Ton-e-pia as observing that "The customary and efficient method of robbing the Indians was in full swing."

What sorts of people were these earlier travelers on the Old Trace? Cotterill describes them as peaceable, leisurely, cheerful, town-dwelling, subsistence hunters and agriculturalists. Lest he be considered a romantic he also finds evidence that their houses were "dirty, flea-ridden, uncomfortable, and unsightly." There was sufficient trade among tribes of the southeastern United States for a language, Mobilian, to have developed, allowing people who otherwise couldn't understand one another to carry on business. Somewhat surprisingly, this interest in commerce appears to have contributed to their openness to early Europeans and later Americans, their subsequent dependence on the products of the trade, and their vulnerability.

But what did they believe? According to Charles Hudson the Native Americans of the southeastern United States had the richest culture of any native people north of Mexico, and the principles of their belief system, strange as many of them appear, were more complete and ordered than our own. Earth was thought of as a circular island suspended from the sky, floating on the waters. And as evidence that some things never change, Hudson thinks that each of the tribes imagined that they occupied the center of the island circle. Preceding and coexisting with This World were Upper World and Under World which, among other things, seem to have represented the eternal dialectics between order and disorder, stability and change, and to an extent, good and evil. The Sun was the primary god, represented in This World by sacred fire, symbol of purity. Sun's brother Moon was also a god but of lesser stature and associated

with fertility. This World was populated by three categories of non-spiritual beings: humans, animals, and plants,
with animals as human allies. There were further subdivi-
sions among the animals and an explanatory mythology.
A host of spiritual beings inhabited the other two worlds
and involved themselves periodically in This World.

An interesting aspect of the oral traditions is that
things of This World that are difficult or less desirable
than they might be are explained as the result of human
malfeasance of one sort or another in "ancient time"
(contrasted with "recent time"). Thus, corn once grew
overnight but now takes a season because instructions
from gods were disregarded. Balance, purity, and order
were emphasized and everything was believed related
to everything else. It was a world of individual responsibility for the occurrence of good and evil and one in
which the community suffered for individual wrongdo-
ing. They recognized that humans had to use Nature
but also that it must be done carefully. Thus, humans
must kill animals to live, but if the killing was not done
respectfully the hunter was at risk for retribution in the
form of disease. In all realms there were proper and im-
proper ways to do things and consequences suitable to
one's behavior.

The cultural and the cosmic were finely integrated in-
ternally and externally. Hudson observes that the belief
system evolved over millennia and was highly effective in
managing individual and communal existence, but it contained a "killing vulnerability": "[...] they were unprepared
to deal with a people whose desire to accumulate property, resources, and land knew no limit, and who recklessly
exploited the earth and its creatures." And so, in the 1830s
came the "removal," forced emigration of thousands of

people westward so that their land would be available for "civilized" usage—largely the plantation economy.

The vulnerability of primitive cultures, whether Choctaw and Chickasaw or contemporary Eskimo, to degradation by representatives of "civilization" or progress has long been curious to me. The process is not always done by force. Hudson says that for southeastern Native Americans it was less military than economic. It seems to me that the vulnerability may lie in their mythologies and accompanying modes of accommodation to existence. Their beliefs ordinarily emphasize a unity of being and the human obligation to respect and adapt to the world as they find it. There is a balance between adapting to and manipulating the natural world, between feeling at one with and apart from it. Thus, belief and action are at once submissive and controlling. And therein may lie a temptation, for "progress" seems finally to offer more effective control, its gods seem more powerful. Is what happens then erosion of traditional belief systems while trying the new and finding their ultimate unfittedness, primitives to the beliefs and beliefs to the primitives? And when the damage is done, the mythology fatally questioned—they are left hanging in the wind?

I have moved north now. It has been an interesting day and a glorious night. I love rain—a good thing since it has kept me holed up most of the day. I know it is nurturant physically whether it blasts down as it did this morning or falls quietly as this afternoon. But gentle, as it ended today, it caresses the earth; subjectively it truly seems a caretaking enclosure. I was the only one here when I arrived at the campground and with the rain I had a pleasant anticipation of sole possession, but soon I felt a solemn sadness as I walked in the mist: aloneness. I think the last six months of mostly being only with my-self have about filled my cup of solitude.

My camp is at the top of a ridge and at the north end—I can see out, down, and around for 300°. The forest here hasn't greened as it had at Rocky Springs, 330 miles south, so visibility through it is still pretty good. In the valleys on either side of the ridge, down some three to four hundred feet, are streams which converge a half mile north. I face west and prepare for night to come. The sunset is a disappointment until I turn to the east and see that it invested all its color there—all the shades of pink. As things darken so do they grow quiet, until I hear what sounds— decisively, it seems—the final bird calling. That leaves only streams sounding (stereophonic) and occasional rustlings in the woods. Not long after the sun goes, Jupiter comes—the sky has cleared to transparency, balance for the day's gray. After Jupiter, in relentless but ineffectual pursuit, comes Orion, and as full darkness arrives so does old friend Pleiades, turned topsy-turvy since its fall term in the east, looking not like a kite but a short-handled, poorly designed dipper. Over my right shoulder hangs the incomparable model, the Big Dipper in the beautiful night sky. Forest and desert alike enchant, and the firmament awes. It also, for empirical souls, offers the best way I know to see the earth turn—in my time watching tonight Jupiter has traveled past three trees and as it arrives at their edge the movement of tree to conceal it, as the Earth turns, is perceptible (with head held absolutely still).

All of this reminds me of my experience at lakeside five years ago when unexpectedly I felt union with water, stars, trees, and Earth. Nothing reveals mystery as the natural world does—from the earth turning to quantum leaping. Our efforts to understand, to chew away at the edges of mystery, are a large part of what gives interest to life, but expanding knowledge does not seem to shrink mystery. Knowledge offers a bit more existential security than, say, the Choctaw and Chickasaw may have felt (I needn't take personally a crow's cawing), but ultimate unfathomability persists, and—sometimes dimly, sometimes brightly but fleetingly—periscopes regions of real meaning. To avoid mystery is to avoid the largest and best part of that. "The way that is known," says Tao, "is not the Way."

I am rocked out of bed this morning by what sounds like a crazed whip-poor-will. Instead of its usual laconic *whip-poor-will,* it is *whippoorwill-whippoorwill-whippoorwill*—like the first child up at summer camp, he wants company. Time for sunrise anyway. The cold morning raises clouds from the streams to look down on. I take the five-mile trail around this section of Trace. Yesterday's rains have every gully awash and flowing to valley-bottom streams. Lovely walk—auditory as much as visual. I arrive back at the campground to find myself again in sole possession. Did none of the other campers want more from here than sleep?

I walked another mile of the Old Trace today. By now that adds to many miles and a lot of imagination set on this old trail. It has been just over two hundred years since the first boatmen traveled this way, a decade under two centuries since the postmen rode it. For the boatmen, it was about a three-week trip to Nashville, half that for the postmen. By the 1820s steam-powered paddle-wheelers on the Mississippi and its tributaries pretty much ended the Trace's importance.

As I walk I try to empty my mind and get a sense

of what it might have been like for those originals to have traveled here. I think I'm not very successful—too much has changed. One easy identification remains, however: the sense of danger one experiences walking through regions where the threat of violence or other crime hangs in the air. I find it on city streets at night; for the boatmen, it was the Old Trace. Disagreement exists as to just how dangerous it was along here, but that many died or were relieved of their trip's profits is unquestioned. Even then, it seems, there were serial killers loose on the land.

Samuel Mason, born in 1750, had fought with apparent honor in the Revolutionary War and subsequently was said to be a solid citizen, until the last decade of that century when, in Robert Coates' dramatic prose, "even now the dark force of the wilderness is laboring at his passions." It began with his arranging for his sons to murder his daughter's prospective husband, a man of whom he disapproved with, perhaps, good reason. For the next ten-plus years he and his gang murdered and robbed their way up and down the Old Trace and around it. There were rumors that a stash of his stolen treasure was buried in the vicinity of Rocky Springs where they had a hideout. The preferred manner of disposing of one's victims during this time, for Mason and others, was disembowelment followed by replacement with rocks and sinking the body in a river or swamp. A psychopath with a weak stomach would have had a short career.

Finally in 1803 Mason was killed west of Natchez by one of his confederates, who cut off his head and took it to town to claim the reward. Unfortunately for the prospective bounty claimer, he was recognized as the long sought and much feared Little (Wiley) Harpe and jailed. He escaped but was soon caught, hanged, and decapitated, with his head mounted on a pole along the Old Trace, presumably as an object lesson for others tempted to mayhem. Similarly, Wiley's older brother, Big (Micajah) Harpe, had also once been a homicidal maniac and met the same fate. It was said of Big Harpe that he regretted but one of his killings, that of his infant son whom, in a rage, he grabbed up by the legs and smashed against a tree. His end came after he thoughtlessly killed the wife and child of a man named Steigal who had been a confederate. Pursued, he was shot in the back and fell to the ground paralyzed. Steigal arrived and, growing impatient with the desultory fashion in which Harpe was dying, began to cut his head off. Big Harpe, a consistent man to the end, exclaimed that Steigal was "a rough butcher, but cut on and be damned!" Steigal left the head wedged in the fork of a tree at Robertson's Lick near the Old Trace. Whether this spate of head removals was an anomaly, I can't say.

I can say that, "land pirates" (i.e., outlaws) or not, the boatmen and probably most of the others who walked or rode this route (except for the occasional Audubon, who painted some of his birds here) were little able to savor or even note its charms. For one thing, the contrast that comes with modern life was missing, as a natural world still abounded. For another, where I cross swamps dry and by bridge, they waded. The Old Trace mostly kept to ridges for just this reason, but it couldn't miss them all. Furthermore, I have no occasion to struggle against wilderness for survival; it is ally, not adversary. And finally, the modern Trace is a far cry from wilderness. Primeval loneliness and fear have been banished from this ribbon of enchanting artifice.

The contemporary irony, and tragedy, appears as failed opportunity. As a national economy, we have far passed survival needs and could now attend to *being*. But mostly, we don't. Instead we drill oil and cut trees as if our next meal depended on it and squander a possible existence unimaginable to the boatmen. In spite of all the changes, in our spirits we are still more boatmen than Audubons.

I am at Meriwether Lewis Campground now, near the Trace's end. In 1809, Grinder's Stand was located here, and at the age of thirty-five Lewis (of Lewis and Clark) died here. No one knows if the bullet that killed him was fired by himself or another. He was traveling to Washington with grievances, but was known to be a moody man given to occasional over-drinking. An early end for a remarkable person.

It is evening again. One of my favorite sounds is a cone falling from a tall pine. It releases quietly, falls through needles and leaves with scratching and rustling sounds, caroms off branches with glancing thuds, and finally strikes ground with a solid, respectable *thump*— nature's equivalent of a bank vault closing. Then it waits.

One of my favorite sights is dead leaves blowing from trees, sailing and falling away. They represent change within continuity, an investment in the future. I stood atop a hill on the Trace, Mississippi's highest point (all of 603 feet), and watched a gust carry several dozen leaves from a tree—probably a gum since they typically hold on to the old until the new march in. They flew out toward the surrounding lowlands, first ascending, then drifting and falling, intent on going a ways. It was an exhilarating sight. I wanted to be among them.

Both of these events represent passing on, death.

There is a confidence to them, belief in the future. Cone and leaf, each return to earth, decompose and flow into it, recompose in new forms. There is reassurance in all this, and satisfaction that it will be my way, too.

Tonight I sit in a great thunderstorm. Rain dances on the camper roof, the windows light up then darken, long thunder rolls. I love thunder, fear lightning—a conflict, since to have the first means to accept the second. I think my fear exceeds my love, but I would not trade the one to avoid the other. They are powers we do not yet understand and will never master. We need that, and them.

Morning comes coldly, thin ice sheeting the damp places. I drive on. The present Trace terminus is at mile 408. At 405 I find a going-away gift—Jackson Falls. In geologic history, the stream that forms this fall approached but did not merge with the Duck River. If it wished to maintain separateness, it came too close. Flooding by the Duck slowly carved a new channel for this stream and one day it quit going north and turned east to join the Duck: "stream stealing," it is called.

I walk down the path along the valley side through floral abundance and at the bottom I stand near the fall's base. Looking up I see rippled water running down terraced black bedrock, wildflowers tracing its edges. The whole setting is utterly beautiful—valley walls, vines and trees and flowers, water, birds, stream coursing to Duck around a slight bend. I return to the top to look east over immaculate green fields and pastures outlined in woods. However do these things happen?

Much of philosophy over the centuries struggles with variations on one question: "Why is there something rather than nothing?" I ask, "Why this something rather than another?" Why this kind of Trace rather than all of the cosmic possibilities for something much less? A mystery with wonderful plot lines.

Now the Trace ends. Part artifact, part Nature, this land speaks to me powerfully. I do not like leaving. It was said in 1831 by one observer of the Choctaws beginning their removal west to Oklahoma that he saw "departing emigrants touching the tree trunks, twigs, and leaves about their homes in token of farewell to these old friends." They knew more of it than I, were embedded and culturally resonant, but, yes, one responds like that.

I turn and follow the Trace south back to Natchez.

— CHAPTER 5 —

Mindful Engagement

*Encounters that I describe as arousing reverent
response are intrinsically spiritual. I mean nothing
supernatural by that; a rich enough experience and
envisioning of natural reality, one that remains
comfortable with the presence of mystery alongside
knowledge, makes appeal to otherworldliness
unnecessary, even foreign. My use of the concept here
is analogous (albeit ordinarily less intense) to that of
many mystics who use it in reference to union with
a transcendent other, but I would rather refer to an
experience of unity or solidarity—sometimes a oneness
with that which is profoundly moving but immanent,
the deep engagement of my essence with another's
essence. That said, for many years I have studied
ancient religious and/or spiritual traditions, especially
Stoicism, Hinduism, and Buddhism, looking for the light
they might shed on reverent experience. The story that
follows describes a piece of this exploration.*

IT WAS THE SECOND DAY of a week-long retreat at a Buddhist
monastery, and my meditation periods were not going
well. Since I had come chiefly in the hope of remedying

my meditative deficits, this was discouraging. The calm and concentration that I sought would not be found. Counting breaths rarely made it to ten before my mind was invaded by monologue and distraction. Reaching ten was a moment of joy, quickly dashed as joy too was distraction and failure. After two to three decades of on-again, off-again efforts at home, and now my third retreat, resignation to evident reality began to set in—I was incompetent at sitting meditation.

Later in the day we met with a monk for meditation discussion. A fellow retreatant confessed frustration, his experience tracking mine: Minds busy as ants at a picnic. I wondered aloud if there might not be other ways leading to realization and described my experiences hiking solo through the mountains and deserts, the times of absorption, of beauty and oneness experienced as truth. A young Scandinavian offered that he found something similar in high mountain skiing: unified self, utterly focused, no distraction. Might not these be parallel ways of knowing, ways at times capable of journeying through serenity and insight toward enlightenment in like manner to sitting meditation?

The monk replied, "No, there is only one way, the way of meditation." I was stunned by his absolute certainty and said no more. But it roused me to intense reflection on my experiences sitting in meditation and hiking mindfully, on how much richer moving through Nature has always been and how transformative since my immersion began 25 years ago. My commitment to the philosophy and practice of Martin Buber's I-Thou relations—in which there are two distinct ways of relating to the world: first as an I to an "It," where things are seen as separate objects lacking inherent value and treated as instruments for other ends, and second as I to "Thou," where we meet others in relations of respect and reciprocity and communion—was remembered as well. That night I dreamed one of those unmistakable dreams where one's subliminal center speaks decisively to his consciousness, to which I suddenly awakened and arose from bed, middle of night, and wrote what I could put words to in my journal. When I came home, I wrote more.

The insight of awakening arises in mysterious ways, on odd occasions, and at surprising moments—as we would expect, considering what and where one is and the obscurities of the path we travel. We recognize awakening when we experience it, wonder at the moment's appearance and passing, and appreciate the teaching.

The Flower Sermon, for example: Buddha prepares to address his followers. White flower held aloft, he turns it between his fingers, looks at the flower, then at his followers. No speech. The monk Mahakasyapa alone smiles knowingly in apparent realization of "the true Dharma eye." No one can say what he realized, but Buddha knew it was sufficient and affirmed its validity.

Another, more recent "sermon" took place on September 7, 1851: Henry D. Thoreau was 34 years old, a man of low (conventional) aspiration but high inspiration. The Universe so interested him that he hadn't time for regular everyday work for fear he might miss something important it had to say. As he did regularly, he walked that early September day lengthily around Concord, through pasture, grove, grain field, and over Tupelo Cliff. He saw more than usual—his Journal entries for the day cover 14 pages. Here is what he realized:

> We are receiving our portion of the infinite. The art
> of life! Was there ever anything memorable written
> upon it? By what disciplines to secure the most life
> [...] I do not so much wish to know how to economize
> time as how to spend it, by that means to grow rich
> [in experience and insight], that the day may not have
> been in vain.
>
> What if one moon has come and gone with its world
> of poetry, its weird teachings, its oracular sugges-
> tions? [...] Suppose you attend to the hints, to the sug-
> gestions, which the moon makes for one month,—
> commonly in vain,—will they not be very different
> from anything in literature or religion or philosophy?

Seemingly just another day around Concord for
Thoreau. Begun in the afternoon, his walk lasted well
into night. Moon, stars, aurora borealis; mosquitoes
and crickets; robin and whip-poor-will; trees and cran-
berries. Only another saunter; he'd covered this ground
many times before. For whatever reason, though, the
voices were clearer this day; he listened, and as we see,
responded:

> The scenery, when it is truly seen, reacts on the life
> of the seer. How to live. How to get the most life. [...]
> How to extract its honey from the flower of the world.
> That is my every-day business. I am as busy as a bee
> about it. I ramble over all fields on that errand, and
> am never so happy as when I feel myself heavy with
> honey and wax. I am like a bee searching the livelong
> day for the sweets of nature. [...] The art of spend-
> ing a day. If it is possible that we may be addressed,
> it behooves us to be attentive. If by watching all day
> and all night I may detect some trace of the Ineffable,
> then will it not be worth the while to watch. Watch
> and pray without ceasing [...]

Thoreau was remarkable for his authenticity, the integrity, depth, and coherence of his ways. Although a highly reflective, contemplative man, as far as I know he never "meditated." But there can be no doubt that his *way of knowing* brought forth awakening from time to time. I invite him into service here to illustrate what I will portray more fully below. I borrow also from Martin Buber's depiction of I-Thou relation and from Buddhist views of mindfulness. I wish to suggest that what I call *mindful engagement,* drawing from each of these sources, may serve as well as meditation, and better for many, as a primary way toward remediated suffering and enlightenment. Beyond desire and aversion, beyond ignorance, one arrives through mindful engagement at realization—and in the doing, finds all entry gates become one.

Mahakasyapa beheld the flower and knew. John Muir came upon a lone orchid as he tramped alone through Canadian swamp and woods in the 1860s. He rejoiced and recognized beauty's singularity and that its occurrence was not contingent upon a human beholder for its value. This particular orchid would almost certainly have died and dissolved back into swamp unknown (to human eyes) had he not wandered by. Beauty was a *sign,* a gate on a path to the wisdom experience of interconnectedness, of interdependency. The last five decades of his life manifested what he had learned.

A year before the passages above, on September 19 of 1850, Thoreau walked and noted just this: "Today I saw a sunflower in the woods." Later in the same day's Journal entry comes "Oh, if I could be intoxicated on air and water!" and "That I might never be blind to the beauty of the landscape! To hear music without any vibrating cord!" Flowers, it seems, regularly provide inroads to awakening for those who are attentive to the wonders they contain.

What I call mindful engagement Buber called I-Thou relation. The three realms of being described by Buber all offer themselves for relational engagement while mindfulness opens the doors of recognition: The fabric of Nature, life among other humans, and encounters with mysterious forms of the spirit. In each of these realms, from time to time, one is addressed and may respond with immediacy and affirmation and know the solidarity of engagement. Reverence, loving kindness, and art are the fulfilling works of each of the realms respectively as entered and engaged mindfully. They are where meaning is discovered.

In zazen (thought-free, absorptive meditation), you sit. In mindful engagement in the first realm, with Nature (with flowers), you move and, with senses enlivened, let fully present awareness shine on both detail and whole. You slow to collect yourself and consider, to contemplate and let sensed meaning and unity sweep through. You experience self as bound up with your surroundings and the Universe. Calmed and clarified, you feel cleansed and know reverence for these gifts received.

The second realm: Engagement with other humans. With or without words, dialogue ensues. For a time, exclusive relation unfolds; fully attentive, self-with-other; something new arises between them, a mutuality that honors otherness while connecting across the inbuilt distance, each including the other in their life space, in their focal concern. One hears, responds, and offers the gift of complete presence and authenticity.

The third: Forms of the spirit. Works of art, music, literature, poetry—these are gifts of the spirit that illuminate our reality. In this realm, you are addressed by an invisible source and are inspired with certainty and an impulsion to make it present, to give the impression received—the "call"—a shape or voice that somehow expresses a realization of its meaning and offers it to others as their own address. You become a medium for a sense of something real and unconditioned that takes form as something conditioned by the form of your expression (art, music, poetry...), which is then available for another to choose a response to.

Right mindfulness supports and composes the two dimensions of meditation. Stabilizing/calming meditation through being present and making present, through affirmation and attentive concern. Insight meditation through looking deeply, understanding, seeing clearly. Mindfulness interpenetrates and connects it all in the unification of concentrated being. Of the four "establishments of mindfulness," perhaps meditation does its most salient work interiorly, with the body, feelings, and mental formations, areas not available for the engagement described here, whose chief work is outside in "the between" of relational meetings. These, too, are subject to meditative attention, but they are there as interior meditative "material" because of the already happened engagement encounters.

Mindful engagement is a relation that incorporates and makes whole its participants as they meet in the *between* of mutual presence, subject to subject, one with another.

Mindful engagement, whenever it arises and lights up relations of self to others, extends beyond toward ultimate engagement with existence, including the realization of non-ego, interdependence, contingency, and impermanence. It is sustained through compassionate relations with all beings and fulfilling actions. It may eventuate in enlightenment, a confirmation of meaning.

Meditation carries me inward, to calm, purify, reveal. Mindful engagement takes me outward, to behold, honor, entwine. Meditation as a way of life, meditative living, must surely take shape outwardly—in the phenomenal world—as mindful engagement.

Mindful engagement rests within the two-part movement of address-and-response, in which words may be present but are ultimately unnecessary. One who is fully present and receptive attends and responds from his or her central being. He or she moves into presence with the flower or landscape, for example, and recognizes its particularity and integrity, honors it, and reaches further toward ultimate engagement with the shared ground of flower and person.

A walk through the Sierra Nevada or an old growth forest, taking this stance, opens one further and deeper: sight, smell, feel, and hearing. You sense the mysteries of plenitude and interdependency, wonder at beauty arisen, and feel yourself one with this earth-pine-water-raven creation. Sometimes moved to tears, always moved in some manner, one's self engages with Self, with being. You come to know in body and mind alike the truth of fullness within "emptiness." Fully engaged you will do no unnecessary harm, will care-take when needed, will know love.

Times like these find one simultaneously present, it seems, both in the ordinary everyday of natural-world happenings and in the extraordinary everyday of something more, of enchantment by mysteries from which the curtain has partially risen.

Does any of this depend upon zazen? Not for everyone, but a meditative or contemplative state of being is necessary: The readiness of slowing, stabilizing, not striving—of establishing presence in the now and presence to the unique and transient earthly formation in which we stand. Not a walking meditation but rather a walking, participative, engaged-with-existence sort of presence.

Thoreau, once again, illustrates this process:

> [September 9, 1851] I am convinced that men are not well employed [at their normal work], that this is not the way to spend a day. If by patience, if by watching, I can secure one new ray of light, can feel myself elevated for an instant upon Pisgah, the world which was dead prose to me become living and divine, shall I not watch ever? Shall I not be a watchman henceforth? If by watching a whole year on the city's walls I may obtain a communication from heaven, shall I not do well to shut up my shop and turn a watchman? Can a youth, a man, do more wisely than to go where his life is to [be] found? As if I had suffered that to be rumor which may be verified. We are surrounded by a rich and fertile mystery. May we not probe it, pry into it, employ ourselves about it, a little? To devote your life to the discovery of the divinity in nature or to the eating of oysters, would they not be attended with very different results?

"Hallow the everyday," says Buber in *I and Thou*. And Shunryu Suzuki: "The true purpose is to see things as they are, to observe things as they are, and to let everything go as it goes." No magic or otherworldliness. One world, two aspects. We go through conditionality on the way to the unconditioned without leaving the world behind.

"To watch for, describe, all the divine features which I detect in Nature," Thoreau continues. "My profession is to be always on the alert to find God in nature, to know his lurking-places, to attend all the oratorios, the operas, in nature." Daily throughout his life Thoreau walked, looked, noted, inquired, and felt himself participant and observant among more than he could ever comprehend, however mundane it appeared to some. Mindfully engaged, he encountered meaning and reality in the details, in the whole.

As I've wondered before, it doesn't seem possible there can be only one way of knowing, suited equally for all seekers. My quarter-century-long study of Martin Buber and the I-Thou relationship combined with regular immersion in the natural world during the same years—these fundamentals of my understanding and experience through which degrees of awakening proportionate to my capacities have arisen—along with my long-time seemingly fruitless meditative efforts; all this suggests that one-way-isms, doctrines of exclusivity from whatever source, miss something crucial about the truths of remediated suffering.

In the *Bhagavad Gita*, Krishna describes for the tormented Arjuna different ways to the "pure heart": the paths of action (selfless service with no attachment to the results), wisdom (understanding reality), meditation (stillness and peace leading to union), and devotion/

love. Inconsistently, he emphasizes one or the other as the most important, but it becomes clear that all are essential. The goal is spiritual realization, the ways intersecting and overlapping. As Buber says of I-Thou relations, they represent parallel lines that intersect in the center, the eternal Thou, and we may add, at the truth of emptiness, the absolute.

Meditation holds a priority position within American Buddhism. Sitting, with its rituals and symbols, the emblematic posture compels both beginner and adept. (How often do we see images of Buddha standing?) Recent discussions of the need for a more "engaged Buddhism" point to "karma yoga" (selfless service without attachment) as also necessary to a realized life and recognizes the risks of meditation when it becomes separation from a suffering world. I seek an inclusive path. Meditation as a way among ways and mindful engagement as another, each and all ways interpenetrated by compassionate action, awareness, and wisdom.

The importance of an inclusive path will show itself more clearly as we move forward in these pages. While reverence may rest on the foundation of a specific attitude toward and experience of existence—via mindful engagement—both individuals and cultures express themselves in a kaleidoscopic array. Branching forth from a common center, pathways diverge and entwine, a linguistic polyglot, on their way to participation and understanding. Experiences of Nature, responses to injustice, and formation of life courses—variable as they will be—are drawn forth and illuminated under the polestar of reality, even as faintly perceived by us limited humans.

II: Home

— CHAPTER 6 —

HOME LAND:
FLORA AND FAUNA

*I wrote this piece about a decade ago. I didn't fully
realize until now that, as I encouraged appreciative
presence in one's home landscape, my own home
was hardly normal. It sits in the Central Texas Hill
Country, is rural without many neighbors, and provides
refuge to hundreds of wild and farmed animals. Not
the* wilderness, *of course, but hardly an urbanized or
otherwise extensively altered place either and considered
by many one of Texas' most desirable areas. Then, last
year, we moved to the North Coast of California with
redwoods in the yard and the Pacific within sight and
sound. In short, I have been fortunate in my chosen living
spaces. It may be easier for me to encourage appreciation
and attentiveness to the place one lives and not just to
more dramatic and less altered places than it would be
for those who are not so fortunate in their habitats, but
the point still holds water: to pay attention wherever
you are; discern its hidden virtues; help it be better; care
about it and join others in caring.*

I AWOKE THIS MORNING AT home thinking about "the outdoors" and what it means to me. My first impulse was to imagine a long backpack in the Sierra Nevada, my favorite place. Away from it all, in the mountains and on the trail: a natural world remote and less blemished, always purer than lived-in, humanized landscapes. I'll always feel that way, but it's a prejudice, understandable though it is, and seeded with potential error.

The error consists in this: delighting in the still relatively unscathed, in its enchanting beauty and reminders of primordially innocent Nature, I may come to depreciate the land on which I walk and work and have my everyday being. I may become careless of its needs and offerings and sufferings, forgetful that it too was once, as Nature advocates are too prone to say, pristine. Tattered and worn, it too is a gift, offering more than I may realize.

So I set aside the envisioned pack, the maps and the imaginings about Sierra backcountry. I arose, looked through the window and up the bluff, and went for a walk. It is January and for the past year it has been dry. We average about 32 inches of annual rain, but 2005 brought less than half that. La Nina is said to be the culprit and she may well impose her desiccating presence on our weather until early summer, say the meteorologists. The air tends to be dusty and the land seems beaten. The grass brown, the dirt too much exposed; the animals are hungry for home-grown forage. We have been months without measurable moisture.

But today they have forecast, with surprising confidence, a one hundred percent chance of rain—a whole tenth of an inch expected in our area. Normally that wouldn't be worthy of notice, but now even meager promise encourages me. Accentuating the positive, drought be damned, I dust off my long-neglected rain jacket and start out. It is overcast and ephemeral drizzle-like mementos of wetter times float downward. It is a great pleasure to feel boots and pants dampen, pathway grow sticky, rocks slick, eyeglasses obscured with fog and raindrops. Rain is always a blessing and even this enfeebled gesture makes me grateful.

We chose the site for our home deliberately. A narrow valley with steep bluffs on either side that climb sixty or so feet up to ridges perhaps 300 yards apart as the birds fly. The now dry Little Blanco River weaves through, hinting that it once carved this vale with surging floodwaters. It's funny that we name these courses "creek" or "river," evanescent as they often are, the only permanence their usually whitened, rocky beds. Probably it should be called the Little Blanco Riverway. It hasn't flowed in almost a year and little enough then.

The bluffs are covered mostly in juniper with a fair mixing of live and red oaks, hackberry and ash. A meadow lies between the river and the south bluff with a dense tree line marking its boundary on the east, scattered trees demarcating its west side. A giant ancient elm is adjacent to the bluff, a sibling of comparable size northwestward, the house situated between them. A few shapely, healthy live oaks dot the meadow. The setting is basin-like and quiet and private since the narrow county road is a half mile to the west and no one lives within sight or sound. It seemed to embrace us when we first entered; we embraced back and made ourselves a home.

This morning I walk eastward past the barn, home to chickens, cats, and food for them and other animal residents. Between barn and house lies a yard fenced into sections, one of which encloses dogs, one for the chickens, and the other shared by the birds with a blind pig. In the meadow are ducks, turkeys, chickens, sheep, and axis deer. Occasionally rheas, donkeys, and mules wander through, every animal rescued from one or another dire circumstance.

I leave the meadow through a cut in the tree line, an abandoned roadway that leads into a second meadow. With time and disuse, the road has shrunk to the trail made by my walks and the four-legged ones coming and going. I follow its familiar curve and across the way east I see movement; from behind a fallen oak come five wild turkeys pursued incongruously by two of our domestic ducks, Mallard-Muscovy mixes, who have recently taken to wandering. I can't imagine what they have in mind beyond what seems apparent—they want to play or visit with the wild strangers, who do not reciprocate the interest. A whimsical sight, these little guys vigorously duck-walking after the strutting turkey hens. They occupy different worlds and I wonder what they think of each other. Two weeks ago, a flock of seven or eight wild turkeys appeared in the meadow in front of the house and cautiously walked toward our gang of resident birds. As we watched, they mingled briefly and then the domestics began hassling the wild ones who chose to leave but in a dignified, dawdling fashion. Occasionally a pair of ravens flies into the red oak outside the kitchen window, whereupon a domestic turkey hen goes up after them as if to chase them away. She approaches, they fly to another limb, she approaches (less gracefully and efficiently), they fly. No one is hurt, and the ravens seem amused.

I always wonder when I see wild and domesticated animals together if they are confused by one another, by their reciprocally anomalous-seeming ways of life. I never feel as if nonhuman wild animals look at humans as one of them—I suspect that they recognize our efforts at transcendence and, whether they figure we have succeeded at that project or not, they accept that we are decisively different and mostly to be avoided. But the wild animals know they share a world and have much in common and, at least those not involved in predatory relationships, act mostly comfortable in each other's presence. But what happens when their worlds dramatically diverge, some remaining wild and others induced into domesticity? Do the wild pity or scorn the others for their lack of autonomy? Do they covet their apparent comfort and conveniences, such as having food brought to them? Do domestics envy the wild ones their freedom and adventure? Or with typical animal grace do they all just see the differences, perplex over them a bit, and then accept the realities without judgment? Animals are a fascinating mystery to me, but I imagine they weren't mysterious in the same way before humans chose to divorce ourselves from Nature, a split that I know still affects me despite my efforts to get past it.

As I move through the meadow, I remind myself to slow down and quiet the inner voice. This isn't a trip intended to get from one place to another; the place of beginning will be the ending. Slower is better, silent mindfulness. The abandoned road approaches the dam across the Little Blanco that it once crossed. Four years ago, we had a weather aberration the opposite of the present one. Mid-summer and a weather system parked above us and let flow—over thirty inches of rain in five days. Little Blanco River showed how she got her name and became a torrent; the sleeping giant awoke. Both this dam and one on the west side of the property were breached. Like a child whose energies can be channeled for a while but eventually must, for her own sake, break out and follow her chosen ways, this river refused any longer to accept damming and resumed its preferred course. It was a wonder to see, as were the days of continuous rain and flowing valley bluffs, the world become water. We thought it possible the rain might never end. For the better part of the following year water flowed down that riverway as a reminder. Its entire course seemed happier.

Rather than follow my trail across the dry stream bed, I turn east and follow its bleached and desiccated way. I've not visited the spring-fed pool in a while and wonder if the drought has exhausted its stamina. I've never known it to dry completely; the fish have hung on through shrinkage and inundation, but this period is surely a test. I find that water remains but less than half the norm, mossy and turbid. When full and clear, fish and water striders busy, shaded as always, this is a meditational place. In survival mode, it seems less so. I spend a few minutes and backtrack, cut up the riverside bluff, cross a clearing, and rejoin the trail beyond where I left it.

I am passing among live oaks now. The property is over 200 acres of wildlife sanctuary, both for the animals who have always lived here and for those who have been brought because there's no other place for them to be. I look up over a rise to the west, for example, and see that I am watched by wolves and wolf hybrids. They live in an enclosure of an acre or so, better than they've ever known considering they were born in captivity and someone tried to make "pets" of them. As toward all the enclosed animals here, I look at them with satisfaction that they have been rescued and are now well cared for. But my stronger feeling is dismay and grief. Nature did not make them to be "cared for," only to occupy their appointed space alongside their wild brethren. They don't belong behind fences, contained and fed by others, forever looking out at a world they no longer participate in. Beyond them, bobcats, then coyotes. Same stories; same feelings.

The generic story of those who live here, covering the 150 primates of various species, mountain lions and other *felids, canids,* bears, exotic birds and reptiles, is this: A wildlife "pet" trade flourishes and many of these animals were drafted into it and when their wildness ineluctably asserted itself they were abandoned or given away. Many have been declawed and/or defanged to make them safer (people want "wild" animal pets but not too wild). Roadside zoos fail, and other zoos have surpluses (that are often "culled," i.e., killed). Animals are confiscated, or research facilities use them up but choose occasionally not to kill them and instead send them to sanctuary. Animals become deranged by their confinement and abuse, and some mutilate themselves—birds who pluck themselves bare, monkeys with intestines hanging out. Many end up dead or worse, remaining in intolerable conditions until they die.

Sanctuaries take in as many as they can and, if they are reputable, give them as nearly natural lives as possible for the time they have remaining. We have unusually spacious enclosures here and do everything possible to encourage species-appropriate relations with their own kind rather than with their human caretakers, so many of the animals actually seem content, although I never deceive myself into thinking their lives are not still diminished compared to their wild and free fellows. One source of my general pessimism about prospects for the natural world (climate change, biodiversity loss, the whole gamut) comes from the knowledge that this treatment of wild animals still remains unexceptionable in society at large. If we have so little respect for these visible, suffering, individual animals, why should we imagine that an upsurge of empathy for other aspects of Nature is likely? Even enlightened self-interest will be slow to assert itself as long as it remains subordinate to economic conceptions of value.

So the sanctuary serves a restitutional function as well as offering something good in itself, as suffering is alleviated and lives saved and improved. Injustice had been done, but now partially remedied.

I walk past the coyotes, some of whom approach curiously (former pets) and others keep a wary distance—thankfully, for these were brought in as orphaned pups and will be released when they are ready. A jackrabbit spooks. He has figured out that the dozen bobcats, half dozen coyotes, and four wolf hybrids who are all within a few hundred yards are captive, so he can forage in an area that his senses would otherwise discourage entering. It's interesting how quickly prey animals learn the efficacy of fences standing between predators and themselves.

A second stream (nameless according to the maps) enters the property at the northwest corner, serpentines its way southeastward and then converges with Little Blanco just below here. For a quarter mile or so north of where I stand it flows, when it flows, at the base of a cliff. I cross the shallow water and walk alongside, cross another converging stream coming from the east (the only one that seems to run always even if minimally), look up at the coyote enclosure, and approach a small dam and the shrinking pool it has captured.

This is a good place to sit for a while. This section of the property is the most isolated—no road reaches it, no wildlife enclosures nearby, down in a valley not visible without effort. The water, tall trees, and seclusion encourage native animal presence, especially birds. Red-tailed hawks nest here and can be seen and heard perched or circling much of the year. Today, as I push through the underbrush, I see a great horned owl whom I'd unknowingly spooked wing away. He's a rare sight though frequent nighttime sound, sometimes in the elm just outside the bedroom window. Farther up the valley where the cliff moves away from the stream is where the ravens congregate. Relative newcomers to this part of the state, we sometimes see a couple dozen at a time circling, often in the midst of vultures. (Hundreds of black vultures hang around the property, a safe place with good pickings when sanctuary carnivores leave leftovers.) As I look off to my right I see a caracara soaring north, a species still rare around here but that seems to be moving its range northward from south Texas. No sooner does he appear than several ravens move in to drive him away. I am very fond of these bright black fellows but would prefer they leave the caracara alone, not that it matters to them.

I walk along a narrow trail on the edge of the sharply descending valley to my left. Because the steep valley walls are dense with trees and underbrush, there's no easy access except when the stream is dry. Through occasional breaks in the tangled foliage I look down at the narrow ephemeral waterway as I hike north. Then, as I near the trail's end, there's an opening and I see what

I only see about once a year. I call them ghost deer because they are so elusive and I can't identify them; sightings are always brief as they hustle away into the brush. Two dark gray creatures, tall and lean. Who they are and where they came from is a mystery, even though I've seen them or their friends for several years, always within this hidden valley. Probably they were left when the previous owner, an exotic animal breeder/dealer, moved out, but it's possible they migrate between our property and the large ranch that nearly surrounds us. Fences across streams are rarely secure. The resident axis deer, who were definitely left by the last owner, are inhospitable to the native whitetail deer and none remain, even though abundant all around us. Somehow the axis have not been able or disposed to evict these few ghost guys. Seeing them surprises and pleases me almost as much as the sight of a black bear in the mountains.

Turning west at the mouth of the valley, I pass another dry pond and then climb to a wide, oval- shaped flat area, probably a third of the property, about sixty acres, where most of the primates and a variety of other animals live. The first I see are black bears, but not the surprising, pulse accelerating variety I come on hiking in the mountains. Rather, it's four old guys who've come from despicable captive situations. Two were held in packing crates in a barn for several years after retirement from an entertainment enterprise. Another had prowled the sidelines on behalf of the Baylor University Bears football team, living in some sort of enclosure on campus between games and seasons. The last had been held in a roadside zoo in New York and almost died from junk food and the Styrofoam containers in which it came to him.

Onward between different species of monkeys on

both sides of the road. Then past mountain lions, a jaguar, African lions. None of the stories about these animals' lives before finding their ways here are pleasant. The amazing thing is that despite the horrors of some of the histories, most of the animals rebound with a resiliency that surely surpasses my own. Formerly isolated primates, for example, with no experience of social life form troops and act in most ways as if back in native habitats. All watch as I stroll through, curious, wary, or just passing the time. Morality tales, lessons to learn, shocked puzzlement: spend a little time here, listen to the stories, watch the animals, take it in. I am always moved in their presence.

I head past the animals and back down into the Little Blanco valley. The promised moisture hangs back; we may not reach even the tenth of an inch. But even in drought an overcast sky and mist are promising and lift the spirit noticeably.

One of the goals I've set for this sexagenarian stage of my life is to look more closely, everywhere but especially here at home where habituation dulls awareness. I suppose I will always most love the Sierra Nevada range, where little effort is needed to pay attention, but I don't live there. Every place is real, every place is one with the whole; it all enlivens me when I am mindful and engaged. In that way, every place is consequential. Each speaks when I listen.

— CHAPTER 7 —

Drought on the Little Blanco River

The period during which I wrote about what was then my home place in Texas was much influenced by two concerns: first, my moving back and forth between home and the Sierra Nevada and reconciling my responses to them, and second, persistent drought and its effects on area plants and animals.

I STAND WITHIN THE DESICCATED channel of what is named the Little Blanco River. It has been a year since water flowed and even then, it was more creek than river. That was September 2010, and eleven inches fell, but in the year since we've received only seven and a half inches; the worst drought in recorded history.

Looking up and down the streambed, I see chalky white surfaces, bedrock that my imagination pictures silently imploring the sky for rain. But that's projection: most dwellers in Nature are adept at patient acceptance of what does or does not come, and this is one of their qualities that I most admire. Even when, as now, I see trees, grass, birds, deer, and small mammals clearly suffering from the heat (it, too, about as extreme as this part of the country has known), I don't picture them complaining. Humans, too, once had respect for fate and its variations, and I believe that the rest of Nature never lost it.

On the other hand, the animals don't just sink into resignation; they try new strategies and some become bolder. We and our chickens notice skunks, opossums, and raccoons coming closer to the barn earlier in the evening than is their habit, and out of protectiveness for the chickens and compassion for the predators we've taken to putting out food and water for them. I probably feel worse than they do about their difficulties, but confess to enjoying the sight of them hanging around on the edges. They are always out there but it's only this inclemency that makes them visible.

Almost bumping into skunks at dusk has encouraged new awareness. Up close, I see how attractive they are, bright white stripe bisecting black back down the spine, long bushy tail, slender body. And like rattle-snakes with their little quantum of poison, these skunks preserve their few tablespoons of oily stink bomb for occasions of real need, which relaxes me a little as they scurry past in the twilight.

Standing in the riverbed, I wonder again how it happened that this little ephemeral waterway gained its lofty appellation. The only occasions during my ten-year experience with the Little Blanco when it acted river-like have been brief periods after very heavy rains. I have seen it foam and rage like high country rivers in the Sierra engorged with spring snowmelt. But after a day or two it has always receded, as if knowing it had exceeded its capacities and was ready to resume its real self, a gently flowing brook easily waded or rock-hopped across. Next after that, rainfall being erratic around here, comes its alter ego, the dry wandering streambed that I now walk.

It requires little stretch to imagine a great river filling this valley a million years ago, or perhaps just rising occasionally and hugely to carve its widening course. Even more recently, I can picture a small river, before so many people came who settled, tapped the aquifer, and the springs began drying up. If this is how it happened, then only the name remains as reminder of former glory, along with those few brief times when it surges.

I see on the county map that the Little Blanco originates only three to four miles west of here. I would enjoy exploring its watershed but fences, absentee neighbors, and "no trespass" signs discourage intrusion. The stream course occupies our property for three quarters of a mile before continuing east and out of the county for about eighteen more miles until it spills into its big sibling, the Blanco River, a real river most of the time, broad and capacious enough to support a state park and a few small impoundments. It arises about ten miles northwest of where the Little Blanco does and flows southeasterly for close to ninety miles to its confluence with the San Marcos River. The San Marcos accepts the offering and then continues southeast another 85 miles to join the Guadalupe River, which carries all that has been gathered and held onward to the San Antonio Bay estuary on the Gulf of Mexico. Little into bigger into bigger and bigger and finally into the really big Gulf when there is water enough to make the complete journey. I've seen flood plain maps that show in blue every little and big waterway (mostly ephemerals) in the county and visually they'd lead you to believe that we were awash and ready to float away or be inundated, but the illusion passes with a stroll along this Little Blanco streambed.

Today I walk west, upstream to limestone shelves that rise to the property line fence and in wet times support flowing cascades. A fifty-yard section of the boundary is formed of a dam, and I look down thirty feet on the neighbor's side to the parched bottom of his carefully dug basin. Rowboats lie upside down and useless on the banks. When the pond is full and the watershed still provides drainage to charge the River, the pond spillway west of the fence delivers a fine flow of water across a broad flat rock surface before it begins its cascades and mini waterfalls. It can be striking, softly plashing and reflecting the clouds even though only a few inches deep over most of its breadth. Onward to the Gulf—water and gravity cutting a fine figure in the mutuality of their primordial relationship.

These falls and cascades descend into a dry pond on our property. When full, it too once leaned against an earthen dam, this one about fifty yards east of the other. The pond was unique around here in the kinds and amount of vegetation it supported. I don't know why but six-foot-high rushes, or reeds, that I call pond grass, were dense (they still are, although now sere and crisp) and made the pond a popular venue for birds, including my beloved great blue heron. The valley bluff forms its south side and is still green with juniper, live and red oak, hackberry, and more, while willows subsist along the absent pond's edges.

Nine years ago we had a week's rain that approached the dimensions of Noah's fabled deluge. Over seven or eight days somewhere between thirty and forty inches fell—I can't be more precise because our gauges filled and overflowed repeatedly after I emptied them. I was daily astonished and remember wondering if it might never end. The Little Blanco River showed then what it could do when called upon to do it. A frothing, tossing, powerful current roared past, sixty feet wide; I could hardly stop smiling and exclaiming, and couldn't have been more surprised if a sedentary friend had suddenly begun running hundred yard dashes at record pace. For several days, we couldn't leave home. Our first venture across was only with the aid of a pitchfork pressed into the river bottom as brace against the current while we carefully waded across.

One result of that great torrent is before me now as I turn from the property boundary and start east downstream through the former pond. The spillway around the dam couldn't answer to what the flooding stream demanded, but instead of being itself washed out, a fifteen-foot-wide area at the dam's opposite end was breached and torn all the way down to bedrock. The River remembered where it was intended to flow and this was precisely that area once again opened to water and light. Now only a small remnant pool remains in the former pond's depths after the River awakens and then subsides, and it still supports that grass.

I continue east down the streambed through the chastened dam's re-opening, a gap that still looks like a wound after nine years. I have mixed feelings about the dam's mutilation. The construction of thousands of these things, big and small, to harness waterways across the country—for hydroelectric power, irrigation and drinking water, flood control and recreation—has damaged untold ecosystems and inundated lands of great beauty. My dismay and disdain are such that I send a share of my charitable donations to groups working to restore two of the worse dam(ned) losses: the Hetch Hetchy Valley in Yosemite National Park, through which the Tuolumne River once flowed unimpeded, and Glen Canyon in northern Arizona and southern Utah which was a Colorado River route on its way to Grand Canyon and then the Gulf of California. Both are now reservoirs, of water but not of the ecosystems and natural wonders which are drowned and out of sight, waiting.

On the other hand, the little pond formed by the dam through whose truncated remains I now walk was a water supply for domestic and wild animals in an often-dry landscape and a home for the remarkable pond grass that I so appreciate. Unnatural though it was, it made for a differently diverse ecosystem and added its own beauty to the property. But I won't defend it and would never have approved its construction. As the hurtling current made obvious, it could not last; the muscle-flexing Little Blanco River would not permit it indefinitely. (Did its generally passive nature foster complacency in the dam builders?) And the result now is that the water course has been distorted and uglied, even while the old streambed has reclaimed its historical path. I smile with satisfaction that Nature overcame the insult and in time will repair the damage.

For a short distance beyond the dam the River has braided a few channels and opened cavities the size of small cars, and then it comes back together among a tumble of rock, tree limbs, and pond grass, a memento of wetter times. The streambed is hard walking now, with boulders and awkward ankle-breaking crevices and trees hanging low. Then it levels and smooths and gently carries on between oak and juniper. A couple hundred yards of this and I cross the dirt road up to our house on the south side of the River.

During the wet year of '09, upstream of the road, for a short while in the spring we witnessed mysterious goings-on in the Little Blanco. After flowing nicely, though not copiously, for a few months, it stopped and began to dry. We mourned the end as we always do when the water quits passing through. But then, as I walked by one morning early, it was at it again, flowing happily along as if nothing out of the ordinary. Later, cessation; then another day and another flow; back and forth it went for ten days or so. No rain, just a willful stream coming out of the rocks this side of the old dam and ending just before it reached the road. What was it: subterranean moon drawn tides, watershed shenanigans, or aquifer readjustments and reassignments answering to its own needs? I don't know, and have been satisfied to accept it as one more of Earth's elegant mysteries.

As I walk now, downstream of the road, the bluff which had bordered the south side of the River has now moved across to the north. On my right I see our garden, house, barn, and meadow, with the fine old live oak in the middle under which our deceased cats and dogs are buried. I continue east, tracing the arid depression, lowest ground in the valley. I come to a three-foot vertical fall that crosses the twenty foot width of the riverbed, climb down and look back, where flowing water undercut the bed and created a narrow cleft, a miniature grotto, which, when the stream rolls over, is curtained behind a waterfall. Four years ago, during a particularly wet summer following many dry months, we spent time here admiring the progression: stream, fall, shallow pool, back to stream. And then something new: as we approached one day a water snake whipped across the pool, and when we looked through the curtain we saw several more of his kind apparently overcome by snakeish sensuality, all intertwined with all, apparently having a ball and oblivious to our voyeuristic enchantment. Day after day we returned and for a few weeks they remained, always a few behind the curtain and others dashing across the pond and hiding under and behind rocks. We were as excited as they and will always remember their presence. And wonder: where did they come from? Where had they waited till aridity turned to precipitation and stream woke up, and how had they found just the right place to prepare their future? How do animals know what they know?

The memory pleases, and I wonder why they've not returned in subsequent wet spells and whether they will ever come back. Even with stream abundant, the spot seems somehow diminished, as it might not if we had never known who'd lived there.

Continuing eastward the River starts twisting, first to the right then sharply to the left and back right. Boulders now dominate and I move to the bank where the going is easier. At that left turn, rushing water has carved a vertical bank starboard twenty feet high, oaks barely holding on and shading it. Then I drift gently back to the right and approach another dam (like the first, built before our time on this land). The pond that once lived here was very different from the one to the west. No pond grass; in fact, nothing obvious grew in it. Rather, this became depository for all the cobbled limestone carved from the streambed and fallen from the bluffs between the two dams. The dried pond's breadth is deep in white stones. And again, identical to the western dam's experience in the deluge of '02, Little Blanco River flexed and reclaimed its natural way. Spillway to the right couldn't manage the flood, and just as before that part of the dam covering the old streambed was breached and bullied away. I walk through the opening and look up fifteen feet to the edge of remnant dam. Earth was piled here a long time ago—a big live oak died shortly after the flood and still bends leeward on the dam.

The riverbed becomes more interesting now. Bluffs on both sides squeeze inward and elevate, trees canopy much of the way, boulders are scattered along—no more easy walking, just rock-hopping and limb-dodging. Fossilized sea creature imprints are common.

And then to my sanctum. Bedrock replaces loose rock and I come to a lip and a five-foot fall into an oval bowl. Bone dry now, but even after river flow shrinks and succumbs, it holds its pool for a time, spring-fed from below, shaded above. It takes many dry months before the level begins to fall. Always there are unexpected little fish. Washed in, presumably, but how did they manage the perilous, battering trip? At those moist times, I come regularly and sit and gaze into the shadowy depths, watch fish swimming casually and then warily, skittish as I shift position above them. Always, I grow somber here. I can't explain why. Its beauty and surprising presence, this hidden little spot, impress themselves on me in a way beyond words. The provocation of it has something to do with the reality it suggests. Astonished, we exist and are both here.

But why solemnity? Other landscapes—the cliffs and falls of Yosemite Valley, the grandeur of Sierra peaks, surging rivers, granite domes—fill me with exaltation, sometimes joyous tears, and the same sense as here of reality beyond understanding. Different responses to the same realization. Maybe it's scale. The others overwhelm and intoxicate me. This pond, even full and teeming and glistening with clear water, feels more an equal, and I know that its existence and mine, amazing as they are, are only temporary.

Today it is parched, dried completely and flaking residue from the last evaporated ounces of disappeared pool. I climb down into it but feel intrusive and crisply move on, out of the bowl and onto the flat streambed going east, now more sand than rock underfoot. Mulleins, with their big fuzzy leaves low set to the ground, obviously find this shady realm appealing and are still green and abundant.

Before I know it, I have arrived at the property line, demarcated by a porous fence across my Little Blanco River. It hasn't a chance of surviving when the next surge comes. The western boundary where I started is open to the world, but this one is closed, unseen. Enshrouded by trees, fence, streambed, bluffs, I could be alone here for as long as I wanted. I make gestures of gratitude and respect and turn up the vanished River toward home.

— CHAPTER 8 —

A LITTLE RAIN

*Preoccupation with drought, its course and effects,
continues; I want to understand it better from a broader
meteorological perspective. And then there's climate
change, our dependence and effects on aquifers, short-
sightedness, denial, and irrationality to consider. A bleak
picture, indeed, which should set us to pondering.*

LATE SEPTEMBER 2011 AND WE'RE about to set a record. If we
finish the month without additional rain, it will complete
a year with only eight inches, a quarter of normal. I have
a chart going back to 1893 for rainfall in this county and
the closest to this year was 10.3 inches in 1954, one of
the years composing the famous Texas drought of the
late '40s to mid '50s. The chart is arranged in calendar
years so there's not strict comparability, but I don't feel
called to go back and make October through September
extrapolations. Suffice that it is dry and surely as dry as
any twelve months since such records have been kept.

Last Saturday, it seemed promises were being made.
Dark clouds from the west, bright lightning, muted thunder, whipping wind: the stage was set—props, backdrops,
lighting—but the actors did not appear, performance

cancelled. A few errant drops cratered the dust and then a still and empty silence moved over us.

On Sunday, more promises; my wife Lynn and I looked at each other and then skyward doubtfully. But it fell, a full three eights of an inch. An attenuated performance but appreciated. It would take days and days of inches and inches to threaten this drought, but by now even mere gestures catch our attention. It fell fast, puddled here and there, cleansed the dusty leaves; in its wake came air scented as I barely remember. Fresh and piquant.

In the true desert, when it rains a smell rises that my olfactories grab, fondle, and hold until it slips away. The scent of creosote and sage, pungent and enlivening: an olfactory five-star gift. This present rain and its trailing bouquet are not quite that, but close. Of the senses, smell, taste and touch are immediate, physically engaged and incorporated in ways that the generally more appreciated sight and hearing are not, though these two are of course prized for the orientation and distinctive pleasures they provide and their apprehensions of more distant stimuli.

Only now, as I make these distinctions that may not survive the rain, am I made to remember how often my sensory capacities do their work and generate their pleasures unconsciously and autonomously. Sources of the material with which I shape a world and fashion my thoughts and gather delights, they labor in the shadows. Sensation, perception, interpretation, conception: I'm a sensory processing device that too rarely becomes fully present and adequately appreciative. It seems remarkable that processes so functional can be so often pleasurable when I bother to pay attention. They are among the cast of characters that transmute survival into meaning.

When will more rain come? We oughtn't do it but how can we not—we impatiently wonder and wait and scan the horizon. Lynn begins each day with the weather forecast. I admonish her, am more comfortable with not knowing, waiting for surprise. But I understand the compulsion.

These weather conditions, extreme heat (over 100 degrees yesterday, late September) and drought are the sort to invite apocalypticism among those who are vulnerable, which thankfully I am not. I've heard more than one person wonder if this is God's punishment for usually unspecified sins. If not the humanized God, though, could it be Gaia's punishing response to our heedless over-reaching? Organisms act to protect and heal themselves and Earth is the all-inclusive organism. Does it go too far to imagine it responding to human imposed afflictions by developing means to slow us down, drain our energies, limit our capacities, and perhaps finally sicken and kill large numbers of us? I remember someone wondering if humans might not be Gaia's self-destructive aspect, arisen by evolutionary accident and now threatening calamity. Or it might be us acting on Gaia's behalf to so deplete the conditions of life that our harmfulness is yanked up short and we make of ourselves a footnote to Earth history while it goes on to repair itself and expunge the signs of our presence, the work probably of a few million years. There are a variety of scientifically well-founded accounts available that make this supposition plausible and even, for the greater good, desirable. Combine increasing population, escalating resource consumption, diminished fresh water supplies, degraded soils, toxified ocean and terrestrial environments, and climate change, and what should we expect?

While I'm not fond of drought, it is what we have right now and worth better understanding. I've learned that there is something called the National Drought Mitigation Center located at the University of Nebraska, which does not really promise mitigation of drought but of its effects through planning and risk management practices. They have a Drought Monitor which rates regions of the U.S. on five levels ranging from D0 (Abnormally Dry) through D4 (Drought—Exceptional). On the map, D4 is colored a livid, almost bloody red and has hemorrhaged all over Texas. More ominously judgmental than I would expect from an academic center, the NDMC refers to drought as "an insidious hazard of nature."

In 1998 Congress, back when it still managed to do a creditable job from time to time, created the National Drought Policy Commission. Along with publishing a report, it defined drought as "a persistent and abnormal moisture deficiency having adverse impacts on vegetation, animals, or people." Such a cool and austere statement—I'd consider it applicable to D1 (Drought—Moderate) but hardly to our present D4, for which I would expect more exuberance: some pulling of the hair and anguished protestation, maybe. There may in fact be definitions of that sort. The Drought Mitigation Center notes that they have found over 150 definitions of drought and some of those might better capture the feel of D4.

I have also been introduced to the Palmer Drought Severity Index (PDSI), which measures what it says it does. Its system ranges from -4 (Extreme Drought) to +4 (Extremely Moist). The area that I inhabit is unsurprisingly -4. I prefer this system over Nebraska's Drought Monitor; it recognizes the symmetry of things and reminds that even a -4 can expect someday to turn the tables and savor the efflorescence of conditions on the +4 side.

Those folks at the University of Nebraska have a wry element in at least one of their scientific formulations. They portray with clever drawings something they call the Hydro-illogical Cycle, which is their way of telling us that drought is natural and universal but that human nature seems to navigate between blithe complacency and rattled desperation as conditions change, which they invariably do but ordinarily so slowly as not to be much noticed until extremity emerges. The cycle begins with rain followed by apathy and then drought; as awareness rises one moves toward concern and then into panic. Six stages in the cycle; I doubt they intended any of this to serve spiritual purposes but it well may as it points toward the value of mindfulness in the present moment, a key aspect of the path toward enlightenment. In this case, recalling the cycle can at least smooth one's movement through the stages and mitigate surprise, promote equanimity, and perhaps even foment a philosophically Stoic disposition toward climatic vagaries.

As one with a keen love of Nature as a whole and individual animals as well, I can't but wonder what strategies wildlife employ at times like this and how well they succeed. We have another series of cyclic interconnections here. Heat and drought impair photosynthesis and pollination; fewer plants survive, which means fewer insects, which lowers seed production. Fewer seeds, plants, and insects cascades into fewer birds and mammals and reduced reproductive success. In short, there is less of everything. And the impact can be international even when other regions enjoy weather normalcy. For example, I've read that one of our favorite birds at the feeder here, Painted Buntings, migrate to Central America, but if fewer survive and reproduce, or they lack the energy to make the trip, there will be fewer who reach their destination, which means that fewer insects will be eaten there leaving more of them to make life difficult for Central Americans. How can we not marvel at the oneness, the entwinement of beings, including ourselves, within this uncanny world?

I walked along our county road a few days ago and was surprised to see a few hardy wildflowers blooming. Most common, actually one of the few in any numbers, is the Dotted Gayfeather. Multiple stems of tiny lavender flowers rise from each base. More striking than its beauty is its very existence under these conditions. There has been so little rain since they last bloomed a year ago; these determined little plants simply bided their time, waited for their appointed month, gasped, and appeared. I expect this of cactus but not of flowers like these. Which is my ignorance; they don't mind aridity, may even prefer it, although I've seen them during wet years in greater abundance. At any rate, I'm so accustomed to plants withering and some dying that I'd forgotten that, no matter what, there are others that will still do their thing when it's time. Thank you, Gayfeather.

There is one other plant I want to recognize. It has numerous names: Texas sage, cenizo, silverleaf, and barometer bush, among others. Several feet high, bushy with gray-green leaves, soft lavender to deep purple flowers—a real beauty when all abloom. What most interests me about this sage, aside from the pleasure of viewing it during its showing-off phase, is what gives it the name barometer bush. A little moisture goes a long way with this provident creature; our last rain of

September (we're in October now) came a few days ago, a full six tenths of an inch. You'd have thought barometer bush had been granted abundance the way it sprang out in full flowering. And it does this frequently, whenever a bit of new moisture comes its way that happens to please it. The unpredictability is enough to surprise, and its floral gifts are always appreciated.

Drought takes you on a slow-motion trip into extremity. How far will it take us, for how long, when will the rain come? Pointless, unavoidable, daily questions. My little chart offers a certain reassurance. Since 1893, as far back as it goes, there have always been scattered dry years, but only during the famed Texas drought of 1947 to '56 has it been the defining characteristic of such a long period. Even then, though, there was variability. Of those ten years, two were slightly above normal (34 inches), four were in the teens or less, and the other four in-between. Average was 22.8, dry but not parched. It was those teen years that killed, and the distance between the up's and down's. But it passed, finally, and Texas returned to its predictable uncertainty, but never as bad since. Unless this year is pointing the way.

I was first exposed to the Sierra Nevada in 1988, fell right in love, and haven't wavered from my commitment. I hope to die somewhere off a trail there. Recently I was reading about the geologic history of the region and learned a new word: megadrought. It arose in answer to a question that I had wondered about just as the scientists had but without their ability to study and answer it. How can the snags with tops above water in Tenaya Lake be explained? According to divers, they range from 25-60 feet below the surface and, like so many trees in these Mountains, are rooted in the granite bedrock.

The answer is that ominous new word, mega-drought. Decades-long droughts of great severity have occasionally occurred in the West and during one that occurred sometime in the early centuries of the second millennium CE the Lake fell so far that Lodgepole Pines had time to move in and spring skyward, only to find themselves inundated when more normal conditions returned. Interesting information in itself, and under current conditions in my part of the world, after only one very bad year, not a prospect I want to entertain. But why not? If it happened then, it will surely repeat itself, especially under climate change disruptions to come. We can only wonder when.

Drought's presence is felt and seen here on the surface where we live. And at times my wandering imagination travels downward toward the aquifer that still yields all the water we need. Not so for everyone, as there are wells going dry, but for us, so far so good. Ever since I was a child I have thought there was something not quite magical but surely mystifying about the presence of vast water deposits deep down below the dirt on which our lives take place. How could good clean water come out of such depths, how did it get there, and how could there be so much?

Growing up in the Panhandle section of Texas, I saw wells dug all over the place to irrigate crops and send water into homes. We floated high above the Ogallala Aquifer. People apparently thought its largesse endless, if they thought about it at all. I remember how farmers would start their wells, turn water into a ditch flowing off to the area to be irrigated, and then feed the water out into furrows running a few hundred yards alongside cotton or grain plants. A wasteful system in itself made worse by the common practice of leaving the fields to go to town or visit a neighbor and so not know when ditches broke and great quantities of water flowed away. Even in my youthful innocence I felt that something wrong was going on when such waste was tolerated.

The Ogallala is known as a fossil aquifer. It began forming 10 million years ago as rain and snowmelt flowed out of the Rocky Mountains toward the east. Coffee brewed today from this water is a mite old. In time, erosion and other geologic processes removed the permeable deposits through which the mountain snow eventually found home in the Aquifer, so its major source of recharge ended. Today, hydrologists estimate that its recharge is on average only about one inch per year. Since about two and a half feet per year are drawn down it doesn't require sophisticated calculation to picture where this story will end. In a few decades, the water will be gone. Today it underlies about 175,000 square miles of eight states between N. Texas and S. Dakota; it is said to be (or to have been) about the size of Lake Huron. Over 90% of it goes for irrigation and agriculture is the heart of this region's economy; something will sometime have to give, and I suspect it won't be pleasant. Short-sightedness and self-centeredness do not make a pretty picture, nor do they foster water wisdom, without which it's hard to envision good times ahead for the Great Plains.

Our home aquifer, the one from which I drank and bathed this morning, is called the Trinity. It runs in a strip from about 50 miles southwest of here northward to the Red River, which separates Texas from Oklahoma. Although not a fossil like the Ogallala, it is slow to recharge; only 5% of rainwater ends up down there. And up here, numbers of people and water wells are rising while the water table falls. Over the next 25-50 years, say the water experts, it will be greatly "stressed." Those whose wells have gone dry think this optimistic. I've seen drawings of what the Aquifer is thought to look like, which to my eyes is on the order of a honeycomb but lacking its regularity of structure. There are pockets of water surrounded by unsaturated formations so that good water here may be absent next door. Horizontal unpredictability is accompanied by vertical and for the same honeycombed reason. Overall, there's a lot of water still but it seems to have the makings for considerable variability neighbor to neighbor and well to well and year to year. And it's not clear that the "water managers" have figured out what to do.

The idea of *finitude* recurs as I think about these things. For some 95% of our *Homo sapiens* history it didn't seem a difficult reality to accept. Finitude was obviously the condition of things and probably seemed as natural as the seasons and the plants and animals that traveled through them, which these ancient ancestors relied upon for sustenance. But modern people think themselves above that nay-saying, defeatist conception. Underlying reality hasn't changed, but our aspirations have and our tools and attitudes. In fact, finitude is never defeated, only postponed or denied. We are finite creatures living finite lives in a finite world ... within an infinite Universe. But the Universe hasn't made available to us its unlimitedness, so finitude remains our condition.

Many want to reject that, whether directly or indirectly, consciously or unconsciously. We seem to imagine ourselves able to fix anything and have everything. I suppose some draw comfort from this. But doesn't it rest on erroneous notions about what gives value to a life, and isn't it delusional? The depletion of our aquifers slowly puts the lie to such ideas. The deterioration of soils, oceans, surface water supplies, and air; climate change and dependency on carbon-based energy sources; mortality itself—we are awash in limitations on our ability to have, and to have without unpleasant consequences.

It seems to me that the closest we might come to pushing the finitude margins outward, and to live consciously and joyously in a Universe that has figured out its own way, is to accept and embrace the limitations and move on toward what's been called limited means on behalf of unlimited ends. Material simplification, meaningful endeavor, lives bounded by satisfying relationships with Nature and fellow humans rather than debt and work, can open a way toward spiritual growth, the only kind of limitlessness available to us.

September passed a couple of days ago. We set the rainless record for one year with only eight inches, an amount that qualifies us for membership in the Chihuahua Desert. I admire and enjoy deserts; they are distinctive and powerful places and I've hiked many a mile through them. But watching what might be the slow transformation of my home place from a land of erratic but generally sufficient moisture into one where it is the exception, and watching trees die and wildlife struggle to hang on will be a test. Finitude imposes itself in a new way and except for the troubling feeling that this may be our own doing rather than Nature's, I wish to honor it and adapt. Or perhaps leave.

— CHAPTER 9 —

RENEWAL

Reverence for this presently parched existence seems
to have paradoxical effects: loving concern for the hurt
endured by the forms of life that make their homes
here combined with acceptance insofar as the drought
and the hurts appear "natural," meaning of course that
they don't arise from the human assault upon climate
and atmosphere. A further paradox arises, as well: a
reverential attitude is not naïve, it understands that
autonomous existence sometimes brings its own hurts
(staying through a hurricane was an excellent reminder
several years ago on Galveston Island), but trust in its
long-term beneficence remains until broken by human
violation—reciprocity betrayed by heedlessness.

THE DROUGHT IS NOT BROKEN but perhaps bent a little.
Historically, this land where I live receives rain in the mid-
thirty inches annually but for two years has gotten less
than half that. Trees and shrubs are visibly stressed and
many have given up and died. The pastures had turned
to dust, the streambeds become mere mementos of
joyous flowing abundance, the wildflowers mostly
absent, and some wells gone dry. Over the past two and

a half weeks, though, eight inches have fallen, and in response seeming miracles have arisen. I was confident that brown would turn green but not clear how since the grass was either eaten or trampled and only a powdery landscape remained, or so said the eyes. But patiently abiding were seeds and roots and in only days new green flora demonstrated its perdurance. Nature's resilience: differently nurturant for different creatures, friendly and reliable. A version of grace, I suppose. Air refreshed, animals pleased, soil damp; how delightful it all is. More like spring than fall, except we welcome slow cooling rather than warming at this season.

Maybe the drought has ended for now, but after two years it will take much more rain to recharge the aquifers. Still, I walked our property this morning and found much to enjoy. The streams are flowing again, except, mysteriously, the one in front of the house. It ran briefly after each of the heavier rainfalls but did not last. I don't remember that it has been more recalcitrant than others after similar rains. Why now?

Too bad about that but who would complain? The others flow and the ponds are full. My favorite little hidden pool, which holds onto its water long after others have dried, had gone empty, but no longer. Its few fish, whose presence there is a recurring mystery, have naturally departed but tadpoles already hatched. I sit on the lip that drops into it at times like this, when the creek is dry but the pool full, and always feel somber. The pool is small, no more than five feet deep, shaped like a twenty-foot-long teardrop, a little sink in the creek's limestone bed, with the channel at this point lying at the base of twenty foot bluffs, shrub and oak finishing the scene and shading it. It seems a place heavy with something, not gloomy but laden somehow with meaning. I don't understand it but am attracted and go there often, although its progressive desiccation saddened me and made the visits less frequent. The place is made for contemplation.

If I were able to speak in the ecstasies of John Muir, this would be the time. The land seems joyous, redeemed, and ready for living even as winter's dormancies approach. Creek beds that were parched only a month ago now host clear, clear water making its circuitous way toward the Gulf, although little is likely to get that far. It flows and calls as it meanders and cascades. Below one of the ponds, where water hasn't reached the overflow channel, it seeps from under the dam. Clarity of air, crispness of morning chill; a flock of ravens flares from a big live oak as I pass by. Purity, that's what it feels like; purity of goodness and nurture.

It occurs to me that when springs and streams dry up, especially as a result of human over-population and over-demand (and anthropogenic climate change) rather than natural vagaries of rainfall and drought, something more is lost than the water. Our innocence, obviously, and I might even say our honor. My local portion of Earth is lessened, its *being* diminished, and the entwinements of life hereabouts, both their spirit and physical well-being, lose essential vitality. Normal variations, extreme ones in particular, have similar effect, but whenever we know that we are the main agent, the loss seems more pronounced, and culpable because not occasioned by Nature. The swift turn from utter aridity to abundant rain, such as this blessed October has brought, draws the contrast distinctly. Humans mostly take—inattentively, ungratefully—without proper reciprocity; Nature mostly gives. One wonders how many losses we will fail to notice as we steadily diminish eco-system richness and health before, too late, grief, alarm, and then action set in?

For now, though, the land is made for pleasure and inspiration. I sense the same feeling in the wildlife and even in our chickens as they range freely over the mead-ow. We really are creatures of Nature, and once again I am reminded.

— CHAPTER 10 —

SNARES

Variability of weather and climate were not all that occupied my attention around the countryside where I once lived. Ranching people characteristically have an instrumental, anthropocentric attitude toward resident wildlife ("pests") and domesticated animals ("food"), and they do not have to look far to find official support for this approach. With an animal rights philosophy and reverential attitude toward both animals and landscape, I have had many occasions to grieve certain human choices around here and how they affect nonhuman members of the community.

I LEAVE THE HOUSE MOST mornings at early dawn, still dark enough that I use a flashlight to ensure that I not disturb a rattlesnake who might lie across my path. Two years ago one of our less cautious dogs took a poisoned hit to the chest here and barely survived. Beyond the gate, I set the light aside as the narrow dirt road reflects twilight and I can step more confidently.

Our home lies on the south side of the 212-acre animal sanctuary and wildlife rehabilitation center that my wife founded in 1977. Then it occupied her house and

109

backyard in San Antonio, but it flourished and grew, and now thousands of native wild animals come through every year for rehab and release and several hundred others (native, nonnative, farmed, and companion animals) make the place home, as do we.

Across the dry bed of Little Blanco River, up the slope, and then I walk west alongside the ten-foot high, chain-link fenced cougar enclosure, within which a dozen of these creatures share about four acres. They are sanctuary animals and will finish their lives here because someone thought they would make good pets or roadside attractions and neither of these dismal enterprises worked out, as they never do from the animals' perspective. Now, usually declawed and some defanged owing to owners' efforts to dilute the wildness of their wild animals, with no possibility of release to wild lands, they are home here, respected, cared for, and given space and privacy to complete their diminished lives with dignity and, we hope, satisfaction.

Through crepuscular quiet and shadow, dawn scents and crispness, I've walked this route for ten years, and still they surprise me. Pounding of cougar pads down the bluff through tall grass straight toward the human prey—I am startled to hear them coming; my breath catches and my heart quickens. There seems no practical purpose for it but they still want to pursue and kill, and only the recollection of intervening fence gets my physiology back to normal as they come to a stop and peer through. Faces blank, impossible to read. Are they reenacting predation, or have they realized the futility of that and charge me just to enjoy the scent of fear and the sport, a diversion for them? Ten feet away I hear the strides paralleling mine and see their shadowed outline as we head west in the near darkness.

Then past the jaguar and the African lions, whose stories are similar to the mountain lions', up the bluff and onward to gate. From here I turn either north or south on the county road and travel about two and a half more miles and then back. Like all roads in this country, this one is bounded by fence on both sides, some four feet high of barbed wire and others eight feet and webbed, "high fence," designed to keep white-tail deer contained along with cattle or goats. I despise them for disrupting the deer's old pathways and their look of imprisoning possession.

A few years ago a banker from a city 200 miles away bought a large piece of land across from us. He prompt-ly enclosed it with high fence and built roads and barns. There's no evidence of intent to live here so it's prob-ably an investment and the cattle and sheep serve to protect his agricultural exemption from property tax and perhaps his image as gentleman rancher during his passing-the-time visits. On one of my morning walks past this property I noticed something not-quite-right at a point where the fence bent inward for a gate. It was a porcupine who had been snared as he attempted to pass under the fence. One end of the wire had tightened to enwrap his torso and the other was secured to a post. He didn't appear injured but the way these things work is that the person who installed the snare would shoot him as soon as he was discovered (today, tomorrow, the day after), assuming he hadn't died trying to escape— just one of the "services" provided by what is called Wildlife Services, a department of the USDA. Before the image-changers got hold of them it was called Wildlife Damage Control. Their website says that they exist "to resolve wildlife conflicts to allow people and wildlife to coexist." In their meaning of this phrase, generally the dead coexist with the living: the no-longer-existing purposeful, vibrant animal and a still existing human who arranged his destruction.

I returned to the sanctuary and asked a couple of our animal caretakers to come out and release the porcupine. Two days later I found a raccoon in a similar situation a half mile up the fence line; we handled it the same way. I wrapped the snares, made of heavy woven wire, around the post and left. A few more days on I noticed the snares had been put back in place and yanked them out. After a couple of repeats of this they were no longer replaced. I began carefully scanning the fence as I walked each morning to see if others had been installed. I noticed that everywhere a little space showed up at the bottom of the fence the "hired hands" had put rocks or logs. It was as if they intended to seal the entire ranch against movement of small animals in or out. Only birds, reptiles, and mice still enjoyed freedom of movement across the fence line.

Why? To protect his sheep against predacious coyotes or dogs, presumably. But there's little evidence coyotes still exist around here due to the prodigious efforts of ranchers to eliminate them. Dogs may be an occasional problem, but are certainly no serious one. And some ranchers use guard dogs, donkeys, or llamas as protectors of their flocks. Lethality is not necessary. Who knows how many small non-target mammals fall victim to this method of predator control?

The way it works is this: the "coexistence manager," i.e., the Wildlife Services employee, finds the little pathways worn by animals up to fences where they dig out enough ground to crawl under and/or bend upward the fence. Look across the road and you see a continuation through the roadside growth and under the parallel fence. I find this evidence of unseen, habitual mammal transit over the countryside intriguing, and wonder about the species and numbers and fantasize hiding behind a bush for 24 hours to observe who's going where. The coexistence manager sees instead a prime place to put his snare. With an opening about the size of the average small mammal's head it catches on his shoulders and enwraps his neck or, if he is lucky, he manages to get a leg or two through before his efforts constrict the coil too tight to escape. Many die of asphyxiation and others just wait, sometimes for days, until the coexistence manager returns to kill them. Regardless of who is the intended victim of this maneuver, many unintended animals die in his place.

One of our dogs is a smallish mixed breed, maybe thirty pounds, product presumably of an unplanned pregnancy—she looks almost like a designer dog. We like to imagine that her stylish mother went slumming one evening and met a cad. We found her along Interstate 10 in far west Texas, the Chihuahua Desert area. She was among a pack of four when we stopped; the others fled and she looked first at them and then at us and decided we looked more promising than the creosote, dry washes, and empty horizon. That was a dozen years ago. Two years later, when I lived alone in a remote area 200 miles north of here, I let her out one morning and she didn't return. After three days she was back with a deep narrow wound encircling her mid-section. She'd been snared and still carries the scar to prove it, fortunate to be alive.

As I jogged southward this morning and reached the top of a rise I looked to the southeast across the hill-and-valley landscape and saw a cumulus alone on the horizon in clear sky. The dawning sun lit the cloud's peak. Nothing out of the ordinary, but for some reason it held my attention and I stopped and watched as the cloud's sloping northern ridge slowly gathered sunlight. Turning Earth and atmosphere slowly rearranged the angles and gradually light and cloud changed, while my attention held steady. Something about it was hard to describe, but the mutuality between sun and cloud, sky and landscape, reminded me of something. It felt fundamental, the self-generated diversity of the material world always standing by, encompassing the farces and dramas concocted by humans taking themselves too seriously. I moved on for another mile, forgot about it as new scenes caught my attention, then turned back north and found it was gone.

I stay alert still for new snares and occasionally find and destroy old forgotten ones, but I've not found an animal caught since that raccoon. What and how strongly I feel about all this depends on how I am feeling about the human species, which varies but usually tends toward disillusionment. If contemporary humans, for whatever reasons, are mostly self-centered and insensitive then the effort to seal a property against wandering wild animals, some of whom may on rare occasion take a predatory interest in one's farmed animals, will be unsurprising even when lethally applied. A few years ago, a bumper sticker showed up on a few pickups around here; it said something to the effect that "And then God created ranchers to protect his Creation." I saw very few of these and none in a long time; the absurdity of it may have been more than even they could bear.

My mother's sister and her husband were Davis Mountain ranchers in West Texas through the middle decades of the last century, and as a child I spent many happy days prowling freely among mountains and up and down creeks on their land. They were good people, as many of their rancher neighbors seemed as well. And religious. But toward the animal representatives of the Godly Creation their goodness did not apply. The cattle and sheep from whose bodies they made their livings were only the most immediate of their victims. "Varmints" were shot on sight, often for no particular reason. More estimable wildlife, such as mountain lions, were trapped and/or shot for competing as hunters of whitetail deer. Black bears were still around the ranch when I was a child but were soon exterminated. It was the 1950s.

Now, a half century later, I live fulltime in Central Texas ranch country where few of the locals are able to make a living from their land. But the attitudes persist. Animal lives mean very little. The history and life habits and intrinsic value of all the species and individual creatures who have occupied this country for eons don't register. We occasionally have coyotes at the sanctuary, usually youngsters brought in from other areas after parents have been killed. We keep them until ready for release, all the while encouraging their continued wildness. At nights I listen to their classic coyote yipping and try to imagine the lives they will lead after they leave. Like the howl of wolves and the whoooing of owls, that yip evokes feeling and fascination. How much deeper and more interesting this land would be if the disappeared wolves and fugitive coyotes were still here speaking to the night. It's a poor substitute when our many dogs summon their own subdued inner wildness and respond to the yipping with atavistic howls, bays, and yips of their own at two in the morning from their places beside the bed.

So, except for those traces of small mammal pathways that I see leading from just inside a fence, crossing the shoulder, disappearing on hardtop, crossing the opposite shoulder, and heading under and away from the other fence, animal history around here is mostly unchronicled. Gone are the black bears, wolves, bison, and mountain lions who impressed our forebears, mostly as threats and competitors and therefore to be extinguished. Just the little traceries of the less threatening creatures remain, the ones that sometimes invite the snarer's trickery.

Human history, though, left more signs and some are visible as I amble this county road. There are said to be over four million miles of public roads in the U.S., paved and unpaved. Having hiked hundreds of miles in remote areas of the country I can attest that roads, often abandoned or rarely used, pop up in the most unlikely places. Ubiquitous road building and road making (through usage) may be as good a marker as any for those who seek clues to the distinctively human. If you have an interest in geology, the cuts made by roads through hills offer the most interesting sites with the least effort. They are a sort of unrobing, like coming upon a person half-dressed. We are so used to surfaces only that to have layer after layer of subsurface revealed cannot fail to intrigue. Eons upon eons are silently registered; you stand on the remains of great events, water and rock and powerful forces below. Time flew, then we built a road through it.

This road I walk on now is mostly silent geologically, but there are clues to more recent times. It winds considerably as it traces hill and valley. It is, as I said, fenced on both sides all along, but occasional properties no longer host livestock—the fences are down, barbed wire in tangles, and old cedar posts decayed and tilted. For a short distance in an area south of here there are a few posts about ten or twelve feet tall, in similar condition, with either phone or electric lines hanging off, unused for a very long time. Not a neatly kept road but I like it that these vestigial signs of past sojourners remain as reminders.

For a little over a mile as I head north, a stone wall, gradually disassembled by time and life, hangs on. It's the only one that was built along this section of road and I wonder about it. The ground in these parts is not typically littered with rocks and there is little farming where they would have been obstacles. The property across the road has no more rocks lying around than I see behind the wall. So they had to be gathered from farther back; the wall was not simply a convenient receptacle for nuisance rocks but something intentional. Limestone chunks, they are mostly the size of misshapen soccer or basketballs with some larger and flat. Skillfully arranged without mortar, considerable labor went into its building. The highest remaining wall is no more than thirty or so inches high. I can't picture cattle or goats restrained long by this slight border; maybe it was for sheep.

Today, a barbed wire fence runs behind it attached to metal posts. Mostly in ruins, the wall travels the road's east shoulder, occasionally at what seems to have been its original height, more often tumbled down to one degree or another, sometimes all the way to its primordial base. Crustose lichen covers much of the rock, and trees and shrubs intrude on the wall, sometimes at the cost of its stability. How old is it? Some of the oaks that took root after the wall was in place are twenty feet tall, and lichen never hurries. Early the last century, I suppose, maybe earlier. Some sections of the road adjacent to the wall are several feet below the land behind it, which reminds me of the Natchez Trace through Mississippi and Tennessee. The identifiable stretches of Trace that remain also sometimes make a lowered corridor, the result of erosion and wear. If this road began as a dirt track, as I'm sure it did, then it too may have slowly sunk before pavement retarded the process. There are places where mammal trails cross and over time the four-legged travelers shoved rock aside to make their passage easier. I see burrows as well. Snakes and lizards and all manner of other small creatures find protection here. Useless now to the landowner, but tenanted by beings who lie back and watch pickups speed past, just as their ancestors watched wagons and horses, cowboys and Indians.

On mornings when the dew has fallen heavily, or sprinkling rain, one of my favorite sights shows up. They're probably always there but it takes moisture to make the diaphanous readily visible. Spider webs, and along this road they are most often of a particular sort which I don't find described in my spider book. Cloudlike, or perhaps more like cotton candy without the density, with diameters ranging from a few inches to a foot. Then they spin into a conical sort of tube that disappears into the grass and underbrush. I know a predator lurks within but usually can't imitate prey sufficiently by vibrating the web to bring him out. All webs fascinate but the diffuseness and rationale of this one are less explicable than the strands of others. As I move along the road early, with dew still heavy, they stand out in their abundance. So much life all around and so much that I don't usually notice.

Two years ago Lynn gave me the complete set of Thoreau's *Journal,* all fifteen volumes. I try to read a few pages every morning and am now on Volume III. Contrary to what I often read about him, I don't consider Thoreau a charming stylist. He is often clumsy and obscure. But he more than makes up for this. He is a fount of sharp aphorisms, of true wisdom, and a model of moving through the world with open eyes, curiosity, and intelligence. He knew that life was intensely valuable and deserved our close attention in all its details. Thoreau was, in short, an authentic human being who knew the *art* of living well, the philosophy of flourishing, as well as pragmatism to help manage the journey. I have the deepest respect for him and would wish to be even half as observant and wise. I read his journal for the pleasure of it and the insights, but maybe most of all because I hope more of his patient and observant manner will flow into me. I have had enough moments of keen awareness in the immediate moment to know that that opens the way—that I do whatever I'm doing at the time better and with more satisfaction, and there's something more. I'm more alive then and enjoy unique delight in that fact.

Which is part of my objection to those snares. I have to imagine that the caught animals find pleasures in existence analogous to my own. Who can rightly deprive any of us creatures of our brief, fascinating tenure here?

III: Being Earth

— CHAPTER 11 —

IN THE BEGINNING

IN THE MID-1980S I BEGAN having experiences that led to what I now speak of as *reverence* for existence. As I've described in the preceding chapters, these arose from encounters in the natural world. I was deeply influenced by Martin Buber philosophically and John Muir's accounts of his Nature revelations. One of my earliest experiences I described in these words:

> Lake shore at midnight—moonless and clear, darkness of silhouettes and stars. Lying on the grass, I survey a sky that seems fuller than usual. Eventually my attention is drawn to Pleiades, that small constellation embedded between Orion and Perseus: trapezoid with tail, a kite hanging in the eastern night. Time disappears for what turns out to be hours while the intimate immensity of space prevails...

> I see the horizon across the lake serrated by trees, lights, and hills with a mile of quiet water between us. Only the occasional phantom wave, stirred by forces unknown, disturbs the surface. Beside me is forest, mostly pine, silent except for rustling of birds. Calls of crickets and frogs suffuse the shoreline. The earth beneath me is firm, damp, and grassy, the air warm...

> Gradually I feel a sense of union with my surroundings. We belong together, the parts fit; there is wholeness, a grounding. Depth of reality is vivid, a presence allowed entry. It happens like this—never enduring, but momentarily filled with certitude and rightness.

I don't recall any preparation for this sort of experience, except unknowingly through my reading and time
spent hiking the forest and hovering around the lake.
What seems normal today was uncharacteristic then; I
had no conscious purpose, no compass, but it felt right
to follow this course wherever it led.

Within a few years it led west to desert country and
the Sierra Nevada. I wanted to work out through deeper
understanding and experience the meaning of Buber's
I-Thou relation with Nature. I resigned my position as
head of a nonprofit counseling center and for several
months immersed myself in western mountains and desert along with time back at that Texas lake. My approach
was to be fully wherever I was, living in a camper and
hiking daily and extensively, to read accounts by others
who had been there, and to write about it in a journal and
essays. It would be a dialogue between the land and me
and with others who had journeyed through it; eventually
it became a chapter within a doctoral dissertation. What
follows is drawn from that study, much abbreviated.

At times, as I reread these pages from so long ago,
I am embarrassed by my naïveté, but I was just starting
on the path that brought me where I am today, and "beginner's mind," as Shunryu Suzuki called it, was all I had
to go on (and in its somewhat matured version, what I
still find firmly in place from time to time). While the journey toward awakening never ends, and occasionally frus-
trates by its elusiveness, it can be reassuring to see how
far along the path one has gone. That it is the most vital
journey I could take, I have never seriously doubted.

The Sierra Nevada

Last night [30 September, 1988] I slept in Death Valley at 100 feet below sea level and then left this morning and arrived in Tuolumne Meadows, 8,000 feet above, early this afternoon. Such different landscapes! Yet the transition between the two as I traveled along, the slow blending and separation, felt like continuity rather than discordance as they met on this good Earth.

My first reaction to this Tioga Pass and Tuolumne Meadows part of Yosemite was simple awe, detracted somewhat by the number of people and my naïve surprise at the degree of campground organization. I didn't expect check-in and check-out times and strict campsite assignment. But that's a small matter. I am humbled and star-struck. How could anyone not respond as John Muir did 120 years ago?

I stood upon a couple of small granite domes today admiring peaks and forest, meadow and river; like Muir I tried to picture the glaciers doing their work, this area having been inundated by ice more than once over the millennia. I am preoccupied with both geologic and nineteenth century history in this place and with the differences between past and present.

A couple of days later I work my way up Lembert Dome, a higher, steeper, more dramatic version of glacial sculpting. Anxiety and exhilaration flood me at the crest, wondering how to get down intact. I envision the glacier slowly sliding through, surmounting and shaping this giant granite wedge thousands of years ago and then Muir bounding over it last century. It is almost too easy to engage with this astonishing place. Muir is an extreme case of I-Thou-ness in a unique area. The more mundane landscapes must reach us as well.

The big black bear that came through the campground earlier was certainly not mundane, although the orange tag hanging from his ear like a price tag on a child's teddy was painfully incongruous with his wild nature. The tag indicates he has been "busted" for previous campground incursions and carted back to remote regions. Unfortunately, he appears not to have gotten the message and his boldness and dependency will probably result in his being destroyed since he represents a potential danger to campers. There is a terrible irony in this—his native aversion to humans was overcome by his attraction to our food and previous innocuous experiences with us and now, having in some sense won him over, we think we must kill him. It would be better to consider him one of the risks of camping; that might help hold the numbers down around here.

In his journal, Muir says that:

> We deprecate bears. But grandly they blend with their native mountains. They roam the rangy slopes in lily meads, through polished glacier canyons, among the solemn firs and brown sequoia, manzanita, and chaparral, living upon red berries and gooseberries, little caring for rain or snow [...] Magnificent bears of the Sierra are worthy of their magnificent homes. They are not companions of men, but children of God, and His charity is broad enough for bears. They are the objects of His tender keeping [...]

And then in *My First Summer in the Sierra,* the account of his first jaunts in these mountains in 1868, he spoke of other mountain creatures: "How many mouths Nature has to fill, how many neighbors we have, how little we know about them, and how seldom we get in each other's way! Then to think of the infinite numbers of smaller fellow mortals, invisibly small, compared with which the smallest ants are as mastodons."

Days pass and I leave for Yosemite Valley where I learn that my store of joyous astonishment at the versatility of granite has not been depleted even though there are more people wandering about here than before in the Meadows. I recognize the dilemma. The Park has to be available to the public, and I hope that their visits will carry over into long term Nature appreciation and respect. Would it be possible in this country, with our pervasively commercial approach to existence, to proclaim that natural areas such as this are special so that minimal human-made intrusions would be permissible, that it is more than scenery, that part of the preferred experience is one of solitude and space, and that there would be no stores, buses, laundromats, and beauty shops, but more spacious environmentally and humanly sensitive campgrounds? Would it?

Muir said this about the Yosemite region:

> The whole landscape showed design, like man's noblest sculptures. How wonderful the power of its beauty! Gazing awe-stricken, I might have left everything for it. Glad, endless work would then be mine tracing the forces that have brought forth its features, its rocks and plants and animals and glorious weather. Beauty beyond thought everywhere, beneath, above, made and being made forever. I gazed and gazed and longed and admired [...]

I followed in his steps and in his responses as I ventured about the Valley and began taking in just how extraordinary this land is. It truly feels like walking through the sanctuary of an immense cathedral. Sunlight from the east streams through trees on clifftops and the mist as if through stained glass; the walls themselves seem carved and sculpted to induce awe. Standing at the base of Yosemite Falls looking up 2,500 feet into the broad face is like standing before an altar. If the world's finest architects were assembled to design the most ethereal cathedral, they would have to arrive at something like this, although probably inferior. I feel humble and privileged while trying to imagine the processes of time, matter, and force that created it.

I sat beside the Merced River for a while and then returned to camp and reread Muir's account of water's movement through this landscape. It always moves me; familiarity only increases its charm.

> How interesting to trace the history of a single raindrop! [...] Happy showers that fall on so fair a wilderness—scarce a single drop can fail to find a beautiful spot—on the tops of the peaks, on the shining glacier pavements, on the great smooth domes, on forests and gardens and brushy moraines, splashing, glinting, pattering, laving. [...] Now the storm is over, the sky is clear, the last rolling thunder-wave is spent on the peaks, and where are the raindrops now—what has become of all the shining throng? In winged vapor rising some are already hastening back to the sky, some have gone into the plants, creeping through invisible doors into the round rooms of cells, some are locked in crystals of ice, some in rock crystals, some in porous moraines to keep their small springs flowing, some have gone journeying on the rivers to join the larger raindrop of the ocean. From form to form, beauty to beauty, ever changing, never resting, all are speeding on with love's enthusiasm, singing with the stars the eternal song of creation.

My, how I love that man.

I move from river to forest. Forests speak of enfoldment and nurturance within vitality while yet rife with death and decay. Fallen trees are as conspicuous as the erect and living. I find comfort and mystery in its embrace. It has its other side, however, as within the arms of a too attentive lover. It is easy to get lost, it can become oppressive, and I sometimes want to escape to where I can see the sky and horizon. At night, I miss the stars. Even so, I spend days hiking and marveling, even adoring, all I see. And then, nowhere near satiation, I have to yield my campsite to another and leave.

On October 12, I find a camp in southern Sequoia National Park, a place to make home for a while. It's a wonderful spot and feels just right. I'm in the foothills so it's warmer, in a long, quietly splendid valley, alongside a stream that flows full and clear.

As I sat next to a pool on the stream after sketching, I began to notice how much more is visible than I ordinarily notice. First I saw reflections, then more reflections, reflections within shadows and reflections within reflections. Eventually I recognized that the entire surface of the water was a mirror for something and with shimmering depths. Almost otherworldly. There is a similar plentitude of other sensations as well when I am attentive. And if true for the senses, what more? I wonder how much I miss.

Another day has passed. These early mornings (it's 5:30) in the dark and chill with only lantern for light, stream for sound, and dog Annie for company have a peculiar comfort to them. A promise of some sort. The sky is at its clearest best; I have come to prefer the morning sky to the evening. Jupiter has moved on, morning star is just above the mountain rim, Pleiades, unrisen when I go to bed, is high above (it's my favorite constellation: compact, subtle, distinct but unimposing). Morning is quiet.

Sun rises over valley rim; it is cool, fresh, and peaceful. Birds call and stream rolls by. Each day feels deeper with calm absorption.

Nature, if we are open to it, leads away from artifacts and the humanized "given," and points to essence and creation, to origins and truth. It reminds that human existence is only recent, was not preordained, and may have been only an accident. It reveals and demonstrates creativity inherent in natural processes. It is continuity, beauty, interconnection. It displaces the human from the altar, exalts life, whispers spirit. Also, it is companionable. Said Muir:

> People who come here ought to abandon and forget all that is called business and duty, etc.; they should forget their individual existences, should forget they are born. They should as nearly as possible live the life of a particle of dust in the wind, or of a withered leaf in a whirlpool. They should come like thirsty sponges to imbibe without rule. It is blessed to lean fully and trustingly on Nature, to experience, by taking to her a pure heart and unartificial mind, the infinite tenderness and power of her love.

Interlude

I'm settling down for a few days to reflect on the mountain weeks since I left home. Here in the camper I have my ancient Royal manual typewriter, an abundance of notes, boxes of books, and time now to begin bringing it all together. I spent considerable time at my lake place for over five years before coming to the Sierra Nevada; it was that time that sensitized me to Nature and brought me to conscious love—this even in the logged forests and abused landscapes of far East Texas.

But I was not prepared for these mountains and how they have affected me, despite all the time I'd spent with John Muir. It almost seems the difference between an adolescent romance and mature love, although I still often feel like an innocent out here.

Notwithstanding the depths of my remaining ignorance, I have learned much from Muir and Buber and, with their help, from these mountains. I need now to bring threads and impressions into greater light and see if there are patterns that I can be more conscious of and draw on as guides. I came to the Sierra because Muir had been here. I have seen the land through his eyes and now mine as well. What have I learned?

Muir immigrated to this country from Scotland in 1849 when he was eleven years old. The family had been settled in the mid-west for many years when he began the wanderings that eventually brought him to California. Beginning with his "thousand mile walk to the Gulf" he wrote copiously in journals and letters and subsequently in essays and books. The evidence of his unique relation with Nature is strewn lavishly among these writings. Buber's I-Thou relation with Nature appears to have been virtually life-long for Muir, but it flowered into ecstasies during his first years in Yosemite. It was decades later when he turned his notes of this early experience into *My First Summer in the Sierra*. Here is some of what he felt:

> It is easier to feel than to realize, or in any way explain, Yosemite grandeur. The magnitudes of the rocks and trees and streams are so delicately harmonized they are mostly hidden [...] The mountains, too, along the eastern sky, and the domes in front of them, and the succession of smooth, rounded waves between, swelling higher, higher, with dark woods

in their hollows, serene in massive exuberant bulk
and beauty [...] To these one's heart goes home, and
the voices of the storm become gentle. Now the sun
breaks forth and fragrant steam arises. The birds are
out singing on the edges of the groves. The west is
flaming in gold and purple, ready for the ceremony
of the sunset, and back I go to camp with my notes
and pictures, the best of them printed in my mind as
dreams. A fruitful day, without measured beginning
or ending. A terrestrial eternity. A gift of good God.

In expressing himself this way, and in others less
exuberantly, Muir gave voice in the clearest way to the
depths of his experience of Nature. He was both earthy
and ethereal and spoke from the very center of pure
reciprocity, he and Nature bound together in Thou-relation. I think I see patterns in how he chose to enter that
relation with the landscape.

First, in his profound receptivity to what Nature presented Muir ventured in with an acute, visionary awareness accompanied by apprehension of profound mystery
at the core of it all. In his journals later in life, for example,
he describes natural objects as multi-sensorially expressive and follows that with description of the synesthetic
perception with which he beheld them. He sometimes
speaks of an innate musicality and melody in landscape.
Jeanne Carr, wife of one of his university professors back
in Wisconsin and his mentor and correspondent for many
years, described his perception as "[...] the eye within the
eye, to see in all natural objects the realized ideas of His
mind." Earthy, ethereal, even spiritual: all in the "dialogue"
he carried on with the natural landscape.

He described perceived phenomena in ways that
at first reading appear metaphoric but that I think he
intended literally. In recounting the "sublimity" and

"majesty" of the Merced River at flood stage he spoke of "seeing and listening at every pore." Later he says of such visions that "They saturate every fibre of the body and soul [...]" Rhapsodizing about Yosemite's beauty in *First Summer* he reports that "one's body is all one tingling palate." The authors of *John Muir: To Yosemite and Beyond,* sounding much like Buber, say of Muir that "One annihilates the self, in truth, in order to read the signs [...]" which he says can be "[...] heard by all who have ears to hear."

Frederick Turner, in his biography of Muir, points out that this perceptivity was initially almost overwhelming to him in the presence of the vast scale and surpassing beauty of the Sierra Nevada. Turner believes that he had a "vision" that demanded an "educated way of seeing": "[...] he had learned enough already to see that all things were related naturally and harmoniously to each other." This puts it well; there was a rhythm for Muir that took in both aspects of natural reality: the objectivity of glacial action, say, along with the wonderful mystery behind it—the movement between fact and vision.

He knew mystery and felt drawn to it.

> He believed in mystery and generally was content not to attempt to trace spiritual matters to their putative sources, recognizing that certain things could never be understood or explained. On the other hand, he was eager to solve certain kinds of mystery, to see how things worked. [...] So in this way he was led from mystery to mystery with a deepening, widening religious awe, one that went far beyond the confines of conventional Christian practice.

Both mystery and Mystery: Muir knew and recognized that in truth they were interlocked and not separable except conceptually. He heard Nature's first voice as aesthetic—awesome, immense, endless arrays of beauty stepping forth to meet him, and he responded with admiration, reverence, and movement into communion. He described it as conversion and baptism.

One day during the summer of 1869 Muir climbed eleven-thousand-foot-high Mt. Hoffman, usually described as the geographic center of Yosemite National Park. From its summit surveying all that lay before him he spoke of feeling "[...] as if Nature had wooingly whispered, 'Come higher.' What questions I asked, and how little I know of all the vast show, and how eagerly, tremulously hopeful of someday knowing more, learning the meaning of these divine symbols crowded together on this wondrous page." As he continued his hike he came upon a woodchuck and the signs of its industry and marveled "what lessons they teach." The next day at Lake Tenaya he saw things "full of divine lessons."

Wolfe, his first biographer, said of him: "The meaning behind the fact, the evidences denoting law, order, creative intelligence, loving design, Muir sought and found in nature's processes."   Nature was both an autonomous presence and a vehicle for enlightenment. His studies of the glacial origins of Yosemite Valley and its environs superseded in many ways those of trained geologists and glaciologists. His was a superb synthesis of science and spirituality.

The second way of conceiving the patterns of Muir's engagement with Nature allows us to better see Buber's central notion of "the between," the living area in which a relational connection forms between oneself and another. In particular, the customary subject-object dichotomy recedes, the picture of unity/kinship/harmony steps forward, and ecological interconnectedness becomes clearer.

We commonly recognize that relational fullness in any area paradoxically requires a sort of self-forgetting. Ego-centeredness negates the possibility of that fullness. Linnie Wolfe says that "[...] when John Muir went into the wilderness, he went in absolute surrender of self and all the concerns of self, to become 'like a flake of glass through which the light passes.'" Engberg and Wesling describe this quality as self-effacement without obliteration. In "A Near View of the High Sierra" Muir put it this way: "In so wild and so beautiful a region was spent my first day, every sight and sound inspiring, leading one far out of himself, yet feeding and building up his individuality." The paradox shows up interestingly here in his movement from "my" to "one" and "his," the use of third person suggesting his transition toward selflessness. I like the way Frederick Turner describes this phenomenon.

> The grand reward was the establishment of an intimacy with a huge block of the natural world. The whole Sierran landscape and skyscape came brilliantly alive for him, spoke to him in syllables and sentences so that at last the old distinctions between subject and object, the knower and the known, the animate and the inanimate, man and the exterior world—all these were dissolved into a mutuality, which is to say a real relationship.

When Muir approached the natural world something happened between him and it and in the relation that arose something more emerged as a transfiguration of man plus land, "a real relationship."

Similar to this blurring of the subject-object dichotomy, the separateness between person and Nature, Muir speaks repeatedly of kinship. In *First Summer,* for example, he realizes that he is "[...] part of wild Nature, kin to everything." Years earlier, hiking in Canada, "I entered at once into harmonious relations with Nature [...] Faculties were set in motion, fed and filled [...] I felt a plain, simple relationship to the Cosmos." At various times he has experiences with animals—dogs, pigs, oxen, muskrat, snake, grouse—where he finds confirmation of the essential oneness of creation. Wherever he opened himself, from anthills to the Universe, Muir emerged with new awareness of Nature's harmonious proportions and processes. He understood that humans had introduced significant disharmonies, but his hope, along with the lessons of his own existence, was that people could learn Nature's "law of cooperation."

Along with ecstasy and lyricism, Muir made scientific observations. In fact, rather than data obscuring his aesthetic and spiritual responses, they often were the vehicle for such response. Knowing the glacial origins of many Yosemite features, for example, did not diminish in the least their wonder and the mysterious feel of what tens of thousands of years of time and physical interactions did to this place. Similarly, the life course of raindrops that I cited earlier he knew as hydrologic fact as well as poetry. Sheep grazing on Yosemite mountainsides produced erosion as well as ugliness. While ecology as a science had yet to emerge, as palpable fact and event it was surroundingly apparent to him: "When we try to pick out anything by itself, we find it hitched to everything else in the universe."

I mentioned earlier that there seemed to me three distinct patterns in Muir's relation with the Sierra landscape and Nature as a whole. The first I described as the awareness of mystery and the feel of wonder. The second focused on kinship in the human-Nature relationship. The third I picture as distinctly spiritual. Martin Buber focused on the human possibility of living a sacramental, or sanctified, existence. Borrowing from Hasidism, he took this to mean that "God can be seen in everything and reached by every pure deed," meaning among other things, that one cannot know God without knowing his works. My own spiritual yearnings and leanings fit neither a Jewish nor Christian framework, but the latter teachings were a major part of Muir's thinking from childhood, although fortunately he was able to move away from the strict Calvinism of his father. Even so, his descriptions often were put in distinctly religious terminology. In an 1873 journal he asked "What is 'higher,' what is 'lower' in Nature? We speak of higher forms, higher types, etc., in the fields of scientific inquiry. Now all of the individual 'things' or 'beings' into which the world is wrought are sparks of the Divine Soul variously clothed upon with flesh, leaves, or that harder tissue called rock, water, etc."

He followed this with a poetic description of interweavings of terrestrial incarnations of the Spirit, what he elsewhere refers to as "instonation." Throughout his writings I find references to Nature as the words of God, as sign-post of the eternal, as that through which and on which God acts, and as manifestation of sacred immanence. In *Son of the Wilderness* Wolfe says that his usages over the years of God, Nature, and Beauty are such as to suggest their identity, and I don't think this overstates it. A variety of pantheism, I suppose, and one that I am drawn to. Beauty was one of the voices through which Nature spoke to him and the relation he formed revealed to him God's ways in this world. Spirit revealing, working, speaking: how else do we know its presence and meaning?

Because of the robust language that Muir commonly used to depict what he saw and experienced, he is
often accused of the dreaded "anthropomorphism."
According to this belief, certain qualities in the world
belong exclusively to humans and to perceive them
elsewhere is to fall into grave error. Muir was very fond
of using language that stressed his identification with
natural objects and activities, language that does not
acknowledge a great barrier between humans and others. And he was neither self-conscious nor apologetic
about it. He experienced streams as glad, loquacious,
enthusiastic, and sad at summer's end. He encountered
"plant people," "winged people," "horizontal brothers,"
and "fellow mortals and neighbors." At other times he
spoke of "human-like enthusiasm," a wilderness "full of
humanity" (not talking about people), and the "humanity" of oxen, being more simply metaphorical here, it
seems to me.

Rather than anthropomorphism in the first exam-
ples, it is probably closer to the truth of Muir's intentions
to see them as analogies used to express his sense that
more goes on in Nature and with animals than is commonly allowed. It was not that he did not accept that
humans were different and even superior in certain respects; he did not wish to denigrate humans while exalt-
ing Nature. But he recognized ways in which some parts
of Nature exceeded human nature. For example, he felt
that Nature's "gardens" were always superior to human
landscaping and that human dirtiness and waste were
nowhere else to be found in Nature. In short, he had a
balanced view of the human and natural worlds and no
need to read the latter in human terms. He also fully
honored the "otherness" of Nature, not as an alien other

or as humanized, but as its own distinctive sphere, one where his words might be the same and their meaning very similar, but whose referents were seen on their own esteemed terms. To have spoken otherwise than this would have been to imagine only a shadow Nature, a Nature arranged anthropocentrically and that was not his Nature (or mine).

No, I propose that Muir's prose be considered description by analogy. It is a commonplace among humans that even the most thoroughgoing empathy cannot succeed in rendering one person's experience transparent to another. In our mutual understandings we inescapably deal in approximations which, fortunately, usually suffice. But how much more difficult is it to comprehend and convey your sense of nonhuman realities? Muir wants to do that, compelled by his deep engagement with Nature. He had to use the only medium available to him—our common language of feeling and desire. To describe a stream as joyous was to acknowledge that in it which resembled that in us called joy, not necessarily joy as a human experiences it but as analogous. Stream joy—I've seen it and know what he's talking about.

I remember the story of Stickeen the dog. He and Stickeen nearly perished on an Alaskan glacier as freezing night descended and they were trapped among deep crevasses. Finally Muir found a narrow, down-looping sliver of ice across a deep forty foot wide abyss. With ice axe he leveled and notched his way to the other side. After much mournful deliberation Stickeen followed, and as he approached the other side's ascending curve:

> He looked up along the row of notched steps I had made, as if fixing them in his mind, then with a nervous

spring he whizzed up and passed me out on the level
ice, and ran and cried and barked and rolled about fairly
hysterical in the sudden revulsion from the depth of
despair to triumphant joy. I tried to catch him and pet
him and tell him how good and brave he was, but he
would not be caught.

I suspect that human and dog consciousness in this
crisis were practically identical but in each's own distinctive form. We cannot finally know, but in this, as in other
less dramatic usages, Muir analogizes, as perhaps in the
final analysis, we humans do with one another.

Both Martin Buber and John Muir point to a unique
experience of the world and, through that, of the "eternal." And both suggest more than that as well. Buber
was content to allow the effects of Thou-relation with
Nature to "remain sunk in mystery." Not so, Muir. He describes the relation with Nature as healing, cleansing,
purifying, enriching, and most important, as transformative: "One touch of nature makes the whole world kin
[...]" This is kinship in the broadest and deepest sense,
temporal and eternal. Engberg and Wesling call it "wilderness thinking": "[...] an ability to perceive wilderness
as value, as ethics, health, discovery, instruction." The
"more than" referenced above becomes direction and
directive, a course of life. I identify with this sense in
both of these my mentors, but Muir is more down to
Earth and this is where I want to be.

The Desert

Night has arrived (17 October, 1988), my first in this
Joshua Tree desert. I was uneasy the first hours here,
my first time camped in desert (except for those few

hours when I arrived in Death Valley on the way to Yosemite) and so very different from mountains and forest
of the Sierra. The desert seems somewhere between indifferent and hostile. Vast, quiet, seemingly uninhabit-
ed, it suggests I may be intruding, but as the afternoon
passed I became more comfortable. Now its quiet is
slightly disturbed by crickets and other nocturnal creatures and its peace absorbing. Surprisingly rich with
flora: cacti, yucca, Joshua trees, juniper, low bushes,
flowers and others I can't yet identify. I am continually
struck by life's intense determination to exert itself in all
environments, as if there existed somewhere an infinite
potential to thrive that searched out all available places
and ways in which to do it.

As I look back over the journal of this trip I begin to
see an underlying theme: given the manifold ways and
places of the relation I-Thou with Nature, it follows that
what is made visible through this is an identification of
human with nonhuman, seeing myself in Nature and
it in me, common interests, shared being. "Deep ecol-
ogists" call it ecological ontology and suggest that we
think of our "self" as, in reality, the world, that apparent
separateness is just diverse expressions of oneness.
This reminds me of the first time I read that the heavy
elements in my body (iron, carbon ...)—without which
there would be no life—originated billions of years ago
in supernovas. I was thunderstruck; the imagery of bits
of my eventual self blasting out of stellar explosions,
speeding through space, becoming part of Earth and
then me was captivating; it shows natural oneness in
the literal material sense.

Aldebaron has risen over the northeastern hills. A
coyote is drinking out of Annie's bowl. We have company.

More than its heat, more than the vast vistas, more than its exotic austerity, the desert is silence. Zoologist John Alcock says it averages about the noise level of a library, but I think libraries are noisier. The silence sometimes has weight that can be experienced physically; sometimes it is an ominous silence without my having the least notion what dangers it betokens. I am still not sure what the desert wants to say.

The coyotes here are a notable presence. Morning and evening they boldly wander the perimeter of the campground and occasionally trot right through. During the night they break into orgies of adolescent-sounding howls and yips, squalling and squeaking nearby over who knows what stimulus. Annie stares intently at them but has shown no desire to attempt a meeting. In *Sonoran Desert Spring,* John Alcock has this to say about meeting animals out here:

> The advantage of the desert is that its sparseness gives us new eyes and the time to focus on what we see. Here there are no jumbled woodlands filled with competing songs of dozens of species, no waves of migrant warblers in the giant treetops to lure a watcher from one bird to the next in a compulsive search for rarer species. On the ridge nothing is common and so each encounter with an animal, even the most familiar species, takes on special significance.

I know what he means although I won't depreciate the significance of any meeting with wildlife, wherever found.

I stand and marvel: rock piles assembled as if by a grand sculptor in some instances, a giant rambunctious child in others, Joshua trees in legions across the valley floor, the austere resplendence of desert flora taking all the space willing to be supportive of each's distinctive needs. It is a different world but tells the same story of life determined to abide. It is also a world that intimidates as no other I have seen. All the natural world has its terms of acceptance but here there are no loopholes. While I experience a sort of Buberian meeting with it, the sense of partnership is evanescent—it seems more a warily tolerant acceptance.

A dirt road forms the campground perimeter. It is a stark boundary between the camper's world within and the desert's world without. I hiked up the adjacent hillside this afternoon and looked back over the valley expanse. The campground, clutching its small area between two rock piles, was virtually swallowed by its surroundings; its presence appeared provisional and temporary. In Tuolumne Meadows when I looked down from Lembert Dome the campground was invisible, absorbed by trees. But I knew it was there and in the mind's eye it seemed fitting. Not so here. I could almost imagine returning and finding no traces. It isn't that the desert seems necessarily hostile, only that it has business of its own to attend to and the human realm does not rank high in its estimation. You might say the same about life forms in general here. They have achieved entente, and while there are casualties, it works. I guess that was also true for the Papago and other indigenes. They didn't contest the desert, only worked with and around it and according to its conditions. Euro-Americans, on the other hand, approached it very differently, as Edward Abbey pungently noted:

> Alone in the silence, I understand for a moment the dread which many feel in the presence of primeval desert, the unconscious fear which compels them to tame, alter or destroy what they cannot understand, to reduce the wild and prehuman to human

dimensions. Anything rather than confront directly the antehuman, that other world which frightens
not through danger or hostility but in something far
worse—its implacable indifference.

Hiking today I left the road and started up the slope
toward the mountaintop. Along the way, in a wash, I
came upon dozens of pine cones, which stunned me.
I could not imagine pine trees here—this is desert. I
continued climbing and reached a point just below the
top where I sat for a while taking in the panorama. As I
descended I saw a squat tree that looked out of place
between two rock outcroppings. The phantom pine had
appeared. Surprised, perplexed, giving all due respect, I
had to take its picture—I assumed it to be the only pine
within hundreds of miles. It was in an arroyo which I
continued to follow only to find seven or eight more, all
but one or two in the same channel. None were pine
tall—instead it appeared their growth had gone into
thickening their trunks and extending themselves later-
ally. They are a mystery in this place (that I resolved back
in camp—my field guide identifies them as pinyon pine,
which has obviously figured out how to survive serious
aridity. How much I have to learn!)

The soil here is not dirt as I have known it. Mainly
a mixture of sand and gravel resulting from decomposition of the rock mountain. It wouldn't seem that anything could grow in it. Yet as I began paying attention
to colors near the desert floor I noticed how much and
how variable its crop is. Every shade of green, many of
yellow, soft red, gray, tans and browns—an abundance
of subtle beauty.

Now it is the 25th of October. I saw stars in a rock
last night. The boulder I am camped beside is a monolith

about forty feet high and 10-15 across at the ground—it looks like a missile tip or half an egg. Igneous rock slowly exfoliating, it is quartz monzonite. The moon is full and as it revolves different crystals catch the beams and become for a time star-like (except for lack of a twinkle). I have also noticed another motion. The moon has been rising farther north each night. Having begun southward from Jupiter four nights ago, it has moved a good 15-20 degrees northward. I am plotting its moves against Ryan Mountain, which I climbed with much pleasure yesterday.

I am increasingly impressed with the purposefulness and busy regularities of this world. Animate and "inanimate" they all have business to attend to, and that people should assume it is all secondary to human purposes is senseless. Alcock noticed as well:

> Each palo verde is a miracle. It would be wonderful to know the complete life story of even one tree on the ridge, to know what coincidences, accidents, and bits of good fortune kept the bruchids, wood rats, and jackrabbits away. How long did the tree take to grow to its present dimensions? What droughts and winds has it experienced? How many wood-boring cerambycid and buprestid beetles have lived within its limbs without killing it? What has been its annual production of flowers and seeds, and how many of its offspring are alive today anchored in the unpromising soil of the ridge, facing the uncompromising sun with the confidence of survivors.

Essayist, novelist, playwright, and poet Mary Austin wondered also what was going on out there among her elusive desert neighbors:

> Probably we never fully credit the interdependence of wild creatures, and their cognizance of the affairs

of their own kind. When the five coyotes that range the Tejon from Pasteria to Tunawai planned a relay race to bring down an antelope strayed from the band, beside myself to watch, an eagle swung down from Mt. Pinos, buzzards materialized out of invisible ether, and hawks came trooping like small boys to a street fight. Rabbits sat up in the chaparral. Nothing happens in the deep wood that the bluejays are not all agog to tell. The hawk follows the badger, the coyote the carrion crow, and from their aerial stations the buzzards watch each other. What would be worth knowing is how much of their neighbor's affairs the new generations learn for themselves, and how much they are taught of their elders.

I am sitting this evening of the 26th day of October in the dark but for lantern light, waiting to see where the moon rises and listening to a Sibelius symphony. In this moment, I am ambivalent about the absence of normal, abundant, flip-a-switch electricity. I miss it for the expected reasons, more than anything else out here, I think; without it I am dominated more than ever by darkness. I am less free, I go to bed earlier, I am constrained to be intimate with a lantern if I want, for example, to write this. On the other hand—the more admired one—I like the need to attend to the waxing and waning of natural light (and heat—this a.m. I willed the sun to surmount my eastern mountain and dispel the desert cold). I am more aware of the natural rhythms and am compelled to recall my context, which is to say, the Universe. I also like the peace and cool and mystery of twilight and darkness.

And Sibelius: I have listened many times to these symphonies on a far better stereo at home. Yet I am hearing them as if with new ears. Their tones and rhythms and moods are far more vivid; they are more appealing, striking, resonant (even with the volume turned low in respect of night).

The moon came earlier than I had predicted—it rose above the ridge just as I was turning off the lantern. And another five degrees or so north. Where will it end? Tomorrow night will be my last here so I may never know. As I sat and pondered it (still full to the casual eye, but appearing fuzzier around the edges, less distinctly and brightly a full circle), I began to wonder about Jupiter—when and where would it appear? To my delight, it arose just about where and when I expected.

It is the twenty-seventh of October now, and early in the morning. The moon is over southwest mountains. It has definitely moved out of fullness, more noticeable than last night. I have never before asked when and where the moon changes phases. But now I know: always, everywhere, slowly.

Mary Austin, too, enjoyed attending to the atmosphere and sky:

> The first effect of cloud study is a sense of presence and intention in storm processes. Weather does not happen. It is the visible manifestation of the Spirit moving itself in the void. It gathers itself together under the heavens: rains, snows, yearns mightily in wind, smiles; and the Weather Bureau, situated advantageously for that very business, taps the record on his instruments and going out on the streets denies his God, not having gathered the sense of what he has seen. Hardly anybody takes account of the fact that John Muir, who knows more of mountains storms than any other, is a devout man.

Days pass, November arrives, and I find myself in a new desert: Organ Pipe Cactus National Monument, an arid-land garden. More about that after some walks through it. For now, I have a sense of the meaning of edenic. I sit drinking coffee, shortly after sunrise, the temperature cool, soft colors, a raven standing watch atop a saguaro a few yards off to the south. Between us a pair of Gambel quail grazes along; a cactus wren inspects the table top three feet to my left, sounds of doves and other birds are abundant. Then a coyote trots in from behind me and scatters the quail followed by Annie charging after him and being halted by her leash. For a few moments, it was all God's creatures together in peace.

Later, having hiked a few miles, "garden" may have been a little strong, but not much. The spacing of plants is closer than at Joshua Tree, the greens are more vivid, and while there seems less diversity—none of the low-lying flowering beauties that provided so much color and so many surprises—there is more abundance, more of each plant. At Joshua only the namesake trees and an occasional juniper and yucca (and the rare pinyon pines) were taller than a person. Here there are saguaro, palo verde, ocotillo, organ pipes, and shrubs nameless to me that reach skyward. Much more verdant overall, but like Joshua Tree a walk through is not so much invited as tolerated.

The colors, sunrise and sunset, have been refulgent, changing, beguiling. Silhouettes of saguaro and ocotillo in every direction. There are moments of quiet confusion when I am not sure if I'm altogether a part of it or alienated—a tension. The beauty, daily evolutions, peacefulness—it seems a model for right being. Only some of the other campers are discordant, and the occasional Air Force jet screaming over with truly alienating power and promise.

El Saguaro is a companionable being. He elicits a

smile, and I involuntarily move in his direction. I would embrace him but for his prickliness. Standing there with chubby arms uplifted, he seems to say, "Yes, you've got the goods on me, but let's not take this too seriously." He is also guilty, far more than any other plant I have noted, of violating the spacing rule. He is commonly seen root-to-root with others, roundly embraced by palo verde branches or waved over by ocotillo. He seems to relish closeness no matter the cost in liquid nourishment although I'm sure he gains something else that compensates—his intimacies are not accidental. If I had a few years to stay and watch there is one relation whose development will be interesting—a major palo verde limb, perhaps three inches in diameter, is resting precisely atop a five-foot saguaro. Some adaptive snuggling is going to be required of these two.

Not satisfied with floral companionship, he also is home to birds. Gila woodpeckers carve out nests, which the saguaro simply grows scars around, and when the Gila is finished, others move in. A most amazing thing to me is watching the birds land on his head—it is amply covered with spines, yet they never seem to stick themselves on landing. According to ethnobotanist Gary Nabhan:

> The special relationship of the Papago with the saguaro cactus characterized their response to an arid homeland. Saguaros are not seen as "separate" life forms at all, not something of an "other," outside world. [...] Papago classify saguaros as part of humankind; a saguaro cactus is "that which is human and habitually stands on earth." It is not, I believe, that saguaros are likened to humans because they often have "arms" coming off their upright trunks. It strikes me that the Papago liken saguaros, *Cereus giganteus,* to *Homo sapiens* because no matter how much they tend to dominate a landscape, they are still vulnerable.

Vulnerable, indeed; John Alcock eulogizes a loss:

> The giant saguaro collapsed and fell during a violent
> windstorm on August 16 [...] If it had been merely big
> this giant saguaro would have been a curiosity, noth-
> ing more. But there was a special symmetry to the
> ancient cactus. It was huge but graceful in its affir-
> mation of life. No person had pocked its flesh with
> bullets, perhaps because no one could fail to admire,
> even revere, this saguaro [...] As it toppled the cac-
> tus carried with it branches of the ironwood tree that
> grew nearby. The majestic permanence of the sagua-
> ro had been a mere illusion, and its death left me
> with a disturbing sense of betrayal.

Love and loss...intimacy and affection arise in surprising
places and between, perhaps, unexpected beings.

When prickly pear cacti die and lie there in the sun
they appear, as with mammals in the same situation,
wretched—as if death and decomposition were a bitter
business. They become black, desiccated, and rather
disgusting. Trees are more tranquil and aesthetic about
the whole thing.

Cholla reproduction strikes me as particularly adventurous. There is certainly ample suspense when a
plant casts its seed to the wind, or through the intestines of birds, but with seeds there is only potential
life—they represent possibility. Cholla, on the other
hand, has already been there. It has felt the wind and
sun and occasional rains while part of the parent plant.
In spite of the security and familiarity of its existence it
takes a leap into the unknown: a segment of limb breaks
off at a joint, hits the ground, and lies there (or is blown a
ways or carried on the unfortunate body of a passer-by
who gets too close). In any event it ends up lying about
unattached to anything, waiting and hoping. The sight

of several of them lying under the parent, some having rooted, others biding their time, is somehow pleasing.

Draco's trapezoid is embedded these nights in the Milky Way. It takes a minute on these clear, black nights to identify it. Binoculars reveal even richer embeddedness. Color changes in clouds beginning and ending the day, the revolving celestial context—everything is perspective, angles, time.

Interlude

Pronuba yuccasella and yucca. Animal and plant: *P. yuccasella,* a small silvery-white moth and yucca, a collection of characteristic desert plants of the agave family; the Joshua tree is one. The relationship between the moth and the yucca is, like legions of others between plant and insect, one of mutualism, symbiosis, *quid pro quo.* In their case the relation is more intense than many others because neither has an alternative: for each, only this particular other will do. Without one another both apparently will die.

But there is more to these two, a feature which makes their relationship utterly unique and introduces wonder of a different order from that of myriad other evolutionary phenomena, however surprising and remarkable they appear. The *Pronuba* moth evinces conscious purpose; it suggests that somewhere along the evolutionary line its ancestors had a rudimentary insight, implemented it, and had it succeed to become an enduring part of their vastly conditioned existence. Whereas in most other plant-insect arrangements the insect secures food and in return accidentally disperses fertilizing pollen or incidentally provides other benefits, our moth has no taste for the yucca—not nectar, pollen, nor other part does she eat. What she does is gather its pollen in a ball under her chin, carry it to a stigma, carefully rub it on, drop eggs nearby on the flower, and disappear. Eventually her larvae emerge, eat a few of the seeds that resulted from the mother's fertilization, drop off to proceed with their accustomed stages of development, and the remaining seeds are dispersed to serve their usual purpose.

Joseph Wood Krutch reacted to this mysterious business in these words: "The staggering question for anyone who has committed himself to 'explaining' nature is simply this: How on earth was such a system of mutual cooperation for individual ends ever worked out?"

Wide-eyed, I second that query, and so, in its variations, do many others. Such astonishment and deep wonder at natural world mysteries sometimes accompanies and other times stimulates one's turn to I-Thou with Nature. As I move from Muir to other, usually less ebullient, participants in deep relation with Nature, I find varied manifestations and backgrounds. As previously mentioned, Alcock is a zoology professor, Nabhan an ethnobotanist, and Mary Austin, who died in 1934, was an essayist, novelist, playwright, and poet. Their sources, experiences, and descriptions of Thou-relation are individual but the referent and the image are indisputably of a single reality.

Unlike Muir, Joseph Wood Krutch had been little touched by the natural world until later in life when he "converted." In 1952 he moved to the desert outside of Tucson, Arizona and remained there until his death in 1970. How did it happen that he moved across the country from New England and began writing natural history

essays? In *The Desert Year* he considers the kinds of response people may have to land and describes what
happened to him on his introduction to desert:

> [...] rarely—perhaps only once, perhaps two or three
> times—one experiences something like love at first
> sight. The desire to stay, to enter in, is not a whim or a
> notion but a passion [...] If I do not somehow possess
> this, if I never learn what it was that called out, what it
> was that was being offered, I shall feel all my life that
> I have missed something intended for me. If I do not,
> for a time, at least, live here I shall not have lived as
> fully as I had the capacity to live.

Thus was he addressed. The final move to Arizona
followed another recognition: "It threatened to become
familiar without being really known and I realized that
what I wanted was not to look at but to live with this
thing whose fascination I did not understand." In the effort to understand he considers that it might have been
the gladness it gave him, its physical charm and warmth,
its beauty, its spiritual element. It was these and something more: "She permits me to suppose that she is expressing something [...] To try to find out what that may
be is the reason I have come once more to look at, to
listen to, and, this time if possible, to be more intimately
a part of, something whose meaning I have sensed but
not understood." He responded with the remainder of
his life, and a measure of that meaning became his.

Among people like Krutch, people who have allowed
such experiences to alter their lives in such a way that the
essential attitude that underlies such relations becomes
determinative, it is impossible not to reflect on what has
happened to them. After an experience similar to my own
at Joshua Tree in which the moon and its changes became
preoccupying, Krutch notes with astonishment, "[...] how

beautiful and how strange it seemed when one took the trouble to be really aware of what was happening." For the next two weeks each night found him out beholding the celestial transitions. Captured by his surroundings, with their newly discovered and surpassing interest, he learned, as Wordsworth and Thoreau before him, "[...] that when the light of common day seemed no more than common it was because of something lacking in them, not because of something lacking in it, and what they asked for was eyes to see a universe they knew was worth seeing."

He spoke of this as having the readiness to look, as "the moment when we are capable of seeing," and as trying "to make oneself a poet." He summarized what had happened in these terms: "[...] what I am after is less to meet God face to face than really to take in a beetle, a frog, or a mountain when I meet one [...] I have noticed them; sometimes they have noticed me; and I am re-minded of something which a certain kind of person is rather prone to forget—that there are other creatures in the world beside himself."

We can assume that Krutch, who was an author and critic before he discovered the desert, entered it with open mind and eyes; he was astonished at what he found and appeared to believe that his meeting with the desert had produced a novel relationship and awak-ened novel capacities within himself. For example, facts and values: the twofold dimensions of his desert quest-ing. He recognized that knowledge fed rather than sated wonder and reverence. He looked and learned: the des-ert scorpion, probably the largely unchanged descen-dant of the first land animal; yucca moths; the desert kangaroo rat, who never drinks, not because he secures sufficient moisture from what he eats, but because he manufactures his own; and cacti, those strange and diverse plants that are indigenous only to our hemisphere. Knowledge was intrinsically valuable to him, and as he learned he also heard the desert speak of its grand underlying mystery:

> If *Dipodomys* never drinks; if the moth desires the candle; if the seed has learned to disregard the wetness of summer while waiting for the wetness of spring; if the cactus has learned to be at home where its ancestors would have perished; who cares? Why, having learned these things, did I not say, "So what" and pass on? The ultimate answer, I think, is to be found only by admitting the mystical element. The reason for my deepest caring does not lie within the scope of biology or even metabiology. One cannot recognize it without being to that extent a mystic.

He denied being a mystic in the usual sense ("At most I have 'intimations,' not assurances [...]"), but his encounter with Nature spoke to him about both quotidian and ultimate mysteries, of values (he admired ecologist Aldo Leopold's "land ethic"), and of Nature's apparent intentions as well as its mechanics. Whatever the precise and probably unknowable nature of his relation, it was surely profound and transformative:

> [...] whether you call the experience infrarational or superrational, it involves the momentary acceptance of values not definable in terms of that common sense to which we ordinarily accord our first loyalty. And to all such experiences one thing is common. There is a sense of satisfaction which is not personal but impersonal. One no longer asks, "What's in it for me?" because one is no longer a separate selfish individual but part of the welfare and joy of the whole.

It interests me that while Krutch did not share Muir's

penchant for language depicting "happy meadows" and "horizontal brothers" he did not reject it. He considered the language we use to describe our experience of Nature worthy of discussion. Other authors, as well, speak in these terms. Austin, for example, speaks of "furred and feathered folk" and "little people." The language we choose is important because it evokes and points beyond the immediate; it communicates on more than a single level. It reflects our identification, or its absence, with the natural world and our beliefs about its essential being. To scrupulously reserve words and categories for humans alone, to eschew the impression of a presumed anthropomorphism, erects a boundary between humans and nonhumans which is rarely valid. I don't need to assert that birds and humans feel the same feelings in the same manner while pointing out the commonalities.

Krutch believed that if it was fallacious to attribute to desert plants and animals such qualities as courage and ingenuity it could only be slightly less so to attribute them to humans. Recalling Wordsworth he agreed that "[...] the joy of nature was older than the joy of man [...]" And more:

> It was Ruskin, of all people, who invented the term "pathetic fallacy" to stigmatize as in some sense unjustified our tendency to perceive a smiling landscape as "happy," a somber one as "sad." But is it really a fallacy? Are we so separate from nature that our states are actually discontinuous with it? Is there nothing outside ourselves which is somehow glad or sad? Is it really a fallacy when we attribute to nature feelings analogous to our own?

It may be that the fabric of existence is (among much else) interwoven with emotionality as a responsive and

expressive potential of all beings in varying manners
and degrees. The glad and the sad, to paraphrase Buber, may be more akin to the air we breathe than to the
blood in our veins.

Edward Abbey, like Krutch, discovered the desert accidentally. As a teenager in 1944 he hitchhiked and rode
boxcars around the country. In 1947, at the age of twenty, he returned to the southwest and lived there until his
death in 1989. As he described it in *Slickrock:*

> [...] I had seen the southern fringe of the canyon coun-
> try. And did not forget it. For the next three years,
> through all the misery and tedium, humiliation, bru-
> tality, and ugliness of my share of the war and the
> military, I kept bright in my remembrance, as the
> very picture of things which are clean, decent, sane,
> and true, what I had seen—and felt—yes, and even
> smelled—on that one blazing afternoon on a freight
> train rolling across northern Arizona.

That ride and its memory set the direction for Abbey's life.

It seems almost universal among people deeply
engaged with Nature to return again and again to the
metaphysical question, "What?" What is it that speaks
so strongly and holds them and leads them on wanting more? Muir speaks of Nature's beauty and harmony
and revelation of God—the experienced reverberations
from inexplicable hiddenness. Krutch is enchanted with
knowledge of multifarious Nature and always finds that
it points beyond to the unknown and unknowable.
Abbey, for all his blustering iconoclasm, travels a similar path: "Far off by the sea, up in the mountains, out in
the forest, down in the silent places in the desert, we can
hear—if we listen carefully—the longest, oldest, deepest
dialogues of all. If we listen."

And he does and he hears, but he isn't always sure

what, or where it comes from. He asks, "What does the desert say?" He understands that desert, like mountain and sea, points to something ultimate, but his ears are attuned primarily to desert rhythms and he thinks them unique. "The desert says nothing [...] [It wears] a veil of mystery. Motionless and silent it evokes in us an elusive hint of something unknown, unknowable, about to be revealed. Since the desert does not act it seems to be waiting—but waiting for what?" Finally, he comes full circle—he accepts the mystery: unassimilable, ultimately strange, the desert yields "[...] treasure which has no name and has never been seen."

Still, though, the urge to understand and to name is irresistible. In *Beyond the Wall* he tries again: The aridity of air, clarity of light, simplicity of landscape, scarcity of man; the queerness of plant life, the hardiness of animal life, the splendor of sundown, the rare miracle of dripping springs. But in the end, "There is something more in the desert, something that has no name. I might call it a mystery—or simply Mystery itself [...]"

This reminds me of Buber's distinction between unfathomable mystery and the mysteries which slowly reveal themselves in response to our attentive address. The world present to our senses and perception is infinitely valuable, in itself and as the necessary occasion for dialogue with things that have no name. Abbey repeatedly experiences this dynamic of two-foldness as he wanders the desert and depicts it as well as he can.

> [...] it seems to me that the strangeness and wonder of existence are emphasized here in the desert, by the comparative sparsity of the flora and fauna: life not crowded upon life as in other places but scattered

> abroad in sparseness and simplicity with a generous
> gift of space for each herb and bush and tree, each
> stem of grass, so that the living organism stands out
> bold and brave and vivid against the lifeless sand
> and barren rock. [...] Love flowers best in openness
> and freedom.

Unity, kinship, interconnection, mutual dependency: all of this we know as scientific data from ecology and evolutionary biology. The kind of relation with Nature that I try to describe turns data into mutuality and experienced reality. Muir, Krutch, and Abbey know this. "We are obliged, therefore, to spread the news, painful and bitter though it may be for some to hear, that all living things on earth are kindred."

In time, inevitably, the unitive web completes itself:

> Through the opening of the canyon I can see the icy
> heights of Telescope Peak shining under the cloud-re-
> flected light of one more sunset. Scarlet clouds in a
> green sky. A weird glow pervades the air through
> which I walk; it vibrates on the canyon walls, reveal-
> ing to me all at once a vision of the earth's slow agony,
> the convulsive grinding violence [...] I am struck once
> again by the unutterable beauty, terror, and strange-
> ness of everything we think we know.

Sometimes he longs for a completion, he and the natural world as one: "Sitting on a hill above our camp, listening to the doves calling far out there, I feel again the old sick romantic urge to fade away into these mountains, to disappear, to merge and meld with the ultimate, the unnameable, the bedrock of being."

Engagement, kinship, merger, and now companionship: Reluctant to stop hiking a canyon at nightfall he notices that "[...] exploring such a place is like exploring the personality of a new friend, a new love." Another time, at midnight on canyon rim, playing his flute: "I stop; we listen to the echoes floating back. I write 'we' because, in the company of other nearby living things—lizards, ravens, snakes, bushes, grass, weeds—I do not feel myself to be alone." While this sort of terminology could seem affectation rather than true experience, the evidence of Abbey's life—forty years in the southwest, often without human companionship, solitary hundred mile hikes through the desert—suggests otherwise; I find it difficult to picture him outside his relation with Nature, the relation that defined him.

What about the dreaded anthropomorphism? Not surprisingly, Abbey opposes both reductionism and personalization in speaking of Nature, the latter because he thought it debased rather than elevated the natural world. As with Muir and Krutch, animal consciousness and feeling and the ethics of human relations with Nature were central concerns. More than once he described "man-centeredness" as a groundless, arrogant, destructive and self-destructive philosophy. In *Beyond the Wall* he becomes intensely explicit:

> The defense of wildlife is a moral issue. All beings are created equal, I say. All are endowed by their Creator (call that God or call it evolution) with certain inalienable rights: among these rights are life, liberty, and the pursuit—each in its own way—of reproductive happiness [...] Human needs do not take precedence over other forms of life; we must share this lovely, delicate, vapor-clouded little planet with all.

> [...] To aid and abet in the destruction of a single species or in the extermination of a single tribe is to commit a crime against God, a mortal sin against Mother Nature. Better by far to sacrifice in some degree the interests of mechanical civilization, curtail our gluttonous appetite for things, ever more things, learn to moderate our needs [...]

He is describing an ecocentric ethic, one that takes with utter seriousness the interests of the nonhuman alongside the human, thus extending the scope of moral significance beyond the usual limits. Human needs and wants, human convenience, are not determinative. From meat eating to tree harvesting to road building, the moral realm stretches outward, along with our estimation of the quality of animal consciousness. Like Muir, Abbey has a "Cousin Bear," and on listening to the calls and observing the behavior of doves, cliff swallows, and frogs, wonders if more is not being experienced and expressed than humans know. After a close encounter with a pair of gopher snakes apparently engaged in a mating ritual, he reflects on what it means:

> I suggest, however, that it's a foolish, simple-minded rationalism which denies any form of emotion to all animals but man and his dog [...] It seems to me possible, even probable, that many of the nonhuman undomesticated animals experience emotions unknown to us. What do the coyotes mean when they yodel at the moon? What are the dolphins trying so patiently to tell us?

What *are* the internal experiences of animals (including domesticated and companion animals, which Abbey seems not to include)? How did the *Pronuba* moth figure out the yucca? We don't know, but with Abbey, I fail to see reason to deny them realities analogous to our own. They clearly have interests and goals and constitute a center of consciousness, and more to the point, mindful relations between us in our realm and them in theirs open dimensions of value and entwinement in which affirmation of their being, along with our own, becomes explicit and inescapable. They, too, we are pleased and privileged to realize, have a world.

Abbey offers us one way to enter and share that world:

> The only right way to get to know this country (any country), the only way is with your body. On foot. Better yet, on hands and knees. Best of all—after scrambling to a high place—on your rump. Pick out a good spot and just sit there, not moving for about a year. (This is my own highest ambition.) Keep your eyeballs peeled and just sit there, through the hours, through the days, through the nights, through the seasons—the freeze of winter, the stunning glare and heat of summer, the grace and glory of the spring and fall—and watch what happens. [...] Pick your place and stay there. You will become a god.

— CHAPTER 12 —

BIG BEND

*The preceding chapter explored several months'
immersion in the Sierras and southwestern deserts
ending in 1989. That period has been followed by regular,
frequent excursions lasting from a few days to a few
weeks each. What follows are short reports from some of
these as I found myself continually drawn to return and
renew, to see what more I could learn.*

IT HAS BEEN FOUR MONTHS since I limped painfully and
prematurely away from the Sierra Nevada. I have treated
the physical problem with acupuncture, homeopathy,
physical therapy, chiropractic, and yoga (although never
so assiduously as this list may imply). Slowly it improved.
Needing to test that, as well as have some solitary time
back in mountains, I have come to Big Bend National
Park. A couple of ten mile hikes with two thousand foot
elevation gains confirm the progress—almost no pain.

Next to Yosemite, I know this place best. It combines my three favorite landscapes: forest, desert, and
mountain. Almost always I camp in the Chisos Basin,
reached by a short road up out of the desert proper but
which still hosts much of its plant and animal life. Agave

(most notably the noble Century Plant: years and years of preparation and finally it launches a stalk twenty or so feet skyward, flowers beautifully, seeds, and dies having been serviced reproductively by Mexican Long-Nosed Bats, hummingbirds, and myriad other birds and insects), prickly pear, cholla and other cacti, sotol, lechuguilla, and a variety of characteristic Chihuahua Desert shrubs and grasses, not to mention a few exotics. Living among these are javalina, cactus wren, roadrunner, western diamondback rattlesnake, Sierra del Carmen whitetailed deer, and their associates and predators. A splendid landscape. The campground is at 5,200 feet with trails extending up into the Chisos Mountains and down into desert.

The Basin has always appealed to me, not least because it truly is a basin, with igneous ridges and intrusion-formed peaks surrounding it and rising over 2,000 feet. Many fine features; I could imagine it a caldera, remnant of one of the multitude of volcanoes that are thought to have been active here a few million years ago. But not so, say the geologists, just an adventitious creation of lava and ash and upraised sedimentary rocks that somehow shaped itself as we see it, or rather, as we see it now, since erosion has lowered and filled and carved in its patient way since only moments after it began. Geology's "deep time" is a reality worth solemn contemplation, particularly for those wondering about the human presence, our arising, our fit, and our probable tenure (about which, it seems to me, there is more to doubt than most people realize). In a similar vein, moving from time to space, last night I pointed binoculars upward at the Milky Way, Pleiades, Jupiter, and a million or so other visible celestial vagabonds. It is solemnizing and enchanting to behold the vast depths.

I'm a different hiker than I once was, and not merely because I have aged. I have learned that in covering fewer miles I see more, and more intently. By reducing mileage by a third I believe I have doubled my awareness.

After 25 years of coming here, I saw my first Big Bend bear yesterday. He sat munching greens on the edge of the trail thirty yards beyond the curve around which I sauntered, saw him, and abruptly stopped, heartbeat and sensoria much aroused. Fat, black, and wooly, a beauty little impressed by my arrival. Not wishing to contest priority on the narrow path and not able to circle because of the steep terrain, I stood silently still and observed. After a few minutes he either finished his snack or became uncomfortable with my presence, turned away and proceeded into the brush.

The story of bears in this area begins with the usual depressing but completely predictable account of human encounters with wildlife, especially of European and American encounters. At the beginning of the twentieth century black bears were common here. By about 1940 they had been hunted and trapped into extinction. And so it remained for forty years. But then a less predictable chapter began, one that astonishes and intrigues. Park literature describes it nicely: "Sometime during the 1980s, a female black bear from the Sierra del Carmen in Mexico started a journey. She descended from the mountain, crossed miles of desert, swam across the Rio Grande, and traversed more desert to reach the wooded slopes of the Chisos Mountains in Big Bend National Park."

Why did she do that? How did she know where to go? Was it like that other mysterious Mexican traveler, the Monarch butterfly, she just knew? Over the millennia there would have been intercourse between these regions and a mental and geographic path remained even after half a century. The aridity of both mountain ranges means that bear carrying capacity is not great, so excess in one may always have led to migration to the other. Currently, a Ranger has told me, they think capacity in the Chisos has been reached, so new journeys south may already be underway. I hope they are careful—the Bush-era "global war on terror" has completely changed the former easy-going quality of this border area; no crossing either way for any purpose is allowed, and it can't be safe even for bear. Nevertheless, the story charms and encourages—autonomous recovery initiated across forbidding landscape and an international border. I am thankful to the National Park that the bears find safety here.

The relatively diminutive madrone is one of my favorite trees, and for one reason especially: she periodically disrobes; she sheds her bark to reveal a deliciously sensual, ivory trunk and branches, so smooth and inviting, so voluptuous, that I can't pass without a few indiscreet caresses. This is her time, and all along the trail she indulges in libidinous display. I am hers. She is also called Naked Indian. My attraction seems to have been shared.

Although not at all uncommon, there's another sight along the trail that after all these years pleases me more than ever—what I call "rock gardens." Whether the size of a wash tub or SUV, these boulders hosting lichen, moss, fern, cactus, grass, flower, tree—in every little crack, crease, and depression—are a joy to behold. Seeds are intrepid travelers, hearty as can be, as even city sidewalk cracks reveal. But up here, they migrate in profusion of species and make homes for themselves in sometimes improbable sites. It's as if some say, "Anybody can do it in dirt, but real men do it in rock." Except there's no pretension; many are as delicate as spider web. Unless their bed goes deep or they are exceptionally pushy, it appears that most of these brave guys reach their limit early and pass on, but until then they share unique little habitats that collectively add wonder to the world.

And the trees: it is mid-November and maple and oak (seemingly a red oak variety called Grave's) are turning yellow, orange, and red. Scattered among pinyon pine, other oaks, green chaparral, ash, hackberry, mahogany, and more, they stand out in wonderful, punctuating color, enhanced in many places by great upthrusts of rock that themselves are multi-colored from lichens and with reddish innards exposed where chunks and sheets exfoliated. And here and there, I see the drooping, or weeping, juniper.

The sum of all this sets a person to thinking, especially his "beginner's mind." Somehow, for some reason, the Universe shaped our solar system and Earth evolved, followed eventually by Chisos Mountains, black bears, Naked Indian madrones, and now *Homo sapiens.* Nature reveals so much of spirit, and now we have consciousness to reflect upon it, be moved and pleased. "Hallow the everyday," says Buber. "Accord yourself with Universal Nature," says Marcus Aurelius. This is world enough for me and has more depth than I come close to understanding. Pay attention, act honorably, love: this will do, here and now.

CHAPTER 13

WATER

THE DAY BEGINS WITH HOURS beside flowing water. My walk starts near the confluence of Tenaya Creek and Merced River. Late June and high country snow is fast disappearing, but the watersheds of both these streams still send down a generous flow, a gift of water always pleasing. Whenever I leave Yosemite I do it with full jugs, which remind me of this place when I thirst.

Today I carry a liter in my pack while its generous source sails past as I walk upstream along the Merced. The trail is dusty, shaded, littered with horse droppings. The flow is rapid in this stretch and frequently squeezed along even faster by bouldered constrictions. It is transparent down to its rocky bed and beautifully reflective of its surroundings, stream flowing over bed of rocks that came from elsewhere and are now settled in place, stabilized though immersed in change. Water astonishes with its protean, forgiving, implacable nature; its manifold generosity seems endless, though humanity sorely tests it.

As I sit watching, it reminds me of a film reel, scene changing slightly with each frame. The ancient notion from Herodotus that "you never step into the same river twice" seems true only in a limited sense. Coursing water

molecules are new every moment but they are only partial representation of river being. River begins in hidden
notches at its highest reaches, gathers, welcomes feeder
streams and snow melt along the way, follows its bed
(which persists even when water has temporarily dried),
and forms a braided continuity from beginning to end.
A whole with shifting aspects. I meet the same changed
river whenever I visit.

Zen master Shunryu Suzuki visited Yosemite Valley several decades ago. In *Zen Mind, Beginner's Mind,*
he speaks of Yosemite Falls and how it recalled for him
streaming water in his Japanese homeland. The book is
a collection of his teachings, and one, "Nirvana, the Waterfall," has special meaning for me. He tells of his former
monastery and of two practices there: when Dogen-zenji
dipped water he always returned the unused portion to
the river from which it came; and when monks washed,
they filled basins only partway and then emptied the water towards rather than away from their bodies.

> This expresses respect for the water. This kind of prac-
> tice is not based on any idea of being economical. It
> may be difficult to understand why Dogen returned
> half of the water he dipped to the river. This kind of
> practice is beyond our thinking. When we feel the
> beauty of the river, when we are one with the water,
> we intuitively do it in Dogen's way. It is our true nature
> to do so.
>
> [...] When we see one whole river we do not feel the
> living activity of the water, but when we dip a part of
> the water into a dipper, we experience some feeling
> of the water, and we also feel the value of the person
> who uses the water. Feeling ourselves and the water
> in this way, we cannot use it in just a material way. It
> is a living thing.

Water *is,* all that it is. I understand what he means.

As I walk the mile and a half toward Vernal Fall the grade steepens, the riverbed narrows, and car-sized boulders become more common. Water is white with turbulence and alive with energy and grace as it surmounts and circles, bends to the rocks' demands. Pools, eddies, chutes, and then at the Fall, splash, spray, mist; I've traveled from silence to cacophony, from transparency to prismatic colors as the rising sun plays with floating droplets.

I don't remember when water began to affect me as it does now. It is difficult even to describe. The material nature of water seems to manifest spirituality more than other substances, even when they assume the most striking forms. Valley wall formations, backcountry peaks and domes, forests and wildflower meadows: there is no resisting any of these, no doubt that they also speak clearly of invisible forces and realities (and of the water that has shaped or fed them). But there is something more in water that eludes me, something totemic.

Since I came upon it a couple decades ago, John Muir's account of raindrops has remained my favorite expression of enchantment with water. He was enjoying his first time in the Sierra Nevada, in the high country north of Yosemite Valley; it was 1868. Thirty years old, he had recently arrived in California after a long trip begun by train from his home in Indianapolis to Louisville, followed by a long walk across Kentucky, Tennessee, Georgia, and into Florida. Laid low with malaria, he delayed for recuperation, and then continued by boat to Cuba where he stayed several weeks. Then to New York to catch another boat which took him to Panama; he crossed the isthmus by train, and then on to San Francisco. Altogether, about a seven month journey.

Muir had been in the mountains six weeks, a time of daily rapture as he immersed in the landscape, when a rain storm thundered in just after noon. "How interesting to trace the history of a single raindrop!" Two pages of lyrical transport combined with deep attentiveness to a raindrop's journey then follow. He reflected that the first such drops, geological ages ago, fell on barren granite, but now they have peaks and domes, forest and garden, to receive them. Some join streams and lakes, falls and cascades, while others merge with meadow and bog where they "[...] creep silently out of sight to the grass roots, hiding softly as in a nest, slipping, oozing hither, thither, seeking and finding their appointed work." Some sift downward through leaf and needle of tall trees while others attach to minerals and shine upon mates drumming through broad-leafed plants of countless varieties.

> Some happy drops fall straight into the cups of flowers, kissing the lips of lilies. How far they have to go, how many cups to fill, great and small, cells too small to be seen, cups holding half a drop as well as lake basins between the hills, each replenished with equal care, every drop in all the blessed throng a silvery newborn star with lake and river, garden and grove, valley and mountain, all that the landscape holds reflected in its crystal depths, God's messenger, angel of love sent on its way with majesty and pomp and display of power that make man's greatest shows ridiculous.

Then the storm ends, "[...] and where are the raindrops now—what has become of all the shining throng? In winged vapor rising some are already hastening back to the sky, [...]" Others are nurturing plants, or if they fell in the highest mountain reaches have locked into ice crystals; and finally many, through spring, stream, and river, make their way to ocean. "From form to form, beauty to beauty, ever changing, never resting, all are speeding on with love's enthusiasm, singing with the stars the eternal song of creation."

No one but John Muir can talk like this and get away with it. This and much more in similar vein are found in *My First Summer in the Sierra*, which was my earliest encounter with the man and these mountains. I was enchanted and have remained so. When we speak of gifts and reciprocity, this exemplifies it in Nature's realm; mindful adoration is its highest expression. Water falls and flows, energizes and sustains, cleans and cools, moves in and out of countless forms and conditions, and yet, so far, it abides and continues to replenish. I sit by the Merced River, honoring the mystic flow.

CHAPTER 14

TREES

TODAY I WALKED. I FOUND much to marvel at and many interesting encounters along the way. I saw a mother quail with several newly hatched chicks and wondered where the father was. A parent of any species tending its young is always strangely engaging, regardless how often we see it. The faith of the youngsters in the parent, the parent's earnest caretaking, the promise of renewal and continuity, even the recognition that many of the young (and old) will be taken by predators—it always brings a smile, and sometimes a few tears, touched as we are by such trust and devotion and presentiment of loss. I am thankful for these things and the chance to share them.

I once embraced a giant pine in order to sniff its bark. Jeffrey Pines are said to smell a bit like vanilla but I couldn't detect it. I did the same another time with an incense cedar, hugging and sniffing. Both times I noticed as I drew my face back an involuntary stroking, hands on tree, gently and spontaneously, as I would a loved person. It seemed at once strange to find myself doing this and yet utterly appropriate. Such strokes are for the doer as much as the recipient; I felt tender toward those trees and their silent, solemn aliveness.

I think it nearly impossible to pay close attention to trees, whether individually or as forests, and not be affected. So steadfast and graceful, they easily become companions. It seems a miracle they can stand so high, waver in the wind and remain upright. A freshly fallen, still living tree evokes sympathy and a frustrated wish to make it right again, while a long dead "nursery" tree supporting a linear stand of youngsters makes me smile and say thanks on their behalf.

As Muir followed sheep up into the Sierra Nevada on his initial foray 141 years ago, he mentioned that "Another conifer was met today—incense cedar, [...]" That "was met" tells me that this was an encounter with another individual life and recognized as such. "I feel strangely attracted to this tree [...] It would be delightful to be storm-bound beneath one of these noble, hospitable, inviting old trees [...]"

Much earlier, in the seventeenth century, an adolescent was converted and brought close to God by a tree. He became Brother Lawrence of the Resurrection, a monk admired for his steady "practice of the presence of God" and his humility. Almost four decades after his conversion he described the experience to his Abbe who recorded the conversation. "One winter's day he saw a tree stripped of its leaves, and considered that sometime afterwards these leaves would appear again, followed by flowers and fruit. He then received a lofty awareness of the providence and power of God which never left him." Well, of course. Who wouldn't react that way if he really thought about it? Botany and theology become one.

J. Krishnamurti seems once to have spent the entirety of several days entranced and enlightened by a tree. At sunrise it became golden leaves filled with life, and "[...] as the hours pass by, that tree whose name does not matter—what matters is that beautiful tree—an extraordinary quality begins to spread all over the land, over the river." Each hour reveals new tree qualities: brightness, liveliness, somberness, quietness, dignity. One may sit in the shade beneath it, "[...] never feeling lonely with the tree as your companion." At sunset finally the tree rests. "If you establish a relationship with it, then you have relationship with mankind. You are responsible then for that tree and for the trees of the world. But if you have no relationship with the living things on this earth, you may lose whatever relationship you have with humanity, [...]" Later, ending a meditation on the human propensity to kill, he extends this thought: "If we could, and we must, establish a deep, long abiding relationship with nature—with the actual trees, the bushes, the flowers, the grass, and the fast moving clouds—then we would never slaughter another human being for any reason whatsoever."

Even Buber, who recognized Nature as a distinct realm of Thou-relatedness without being very comfortable there himself, spoke about trees. He knew they could be "It," a species, a botanical member of an ecosystem, just lumber. "In all this the tree remains my object, [...] It can, however, also come about, if I have both will and grace, that in considering the tree I become bound up in relation to it." He writes, "The tree is no impression, no play of my imagination, no value depending on my mood; but it is bodied over against me and has to do with me, as I with it—only in a different way."

To paraphrase an old television commercial, "These are not your father's trees." (The vast majority of those have been clear-cut.) But they are nevertheless real, and full of the possibility of connection. I have been to the forest, and with Muir and the others, I have met these trees.

— CHAPTER 15 —

STORM

I HAVE MOVED CAMP AND this morning caught a ride to where Porcupine Creek intersects Tioga Road, several miles north of the Valley. Fourteen miles hiked and a late afternoon return to camp. I'd have stayed out longer but storms rolled in at noon.

I was high on North Dome preoccupied with seeing everything—far, near, down into the Valley—when a booming thunderclap shook me. I moved back off the Dome into a rocky pocket with a perfect view of Half Dome, ate lunch and watched a hawk glide and circle between the two Domes, which seem about a mile apart, though estimating distance is tricky at this scale. I think these birds often fly like this for the pleasure of it, just as I hike for pleasure, and we both are responding to the spirit of the place. I walked a little under five miles through forest to get here from my drop-off and then west through deeper forest about the same distance to Upper Yosemite Fall. The trail crossed several charming little streams in miniature valleys. One in particular made home for a host of ferns and delicate flowers. I stopped to take it in, but thunder rolled loud and close, so I left sooner than I wanted.

A mile from the Fall rain whipped in carrying bits of sleet. I saw streak lightning to the north only a couple miles away and heading south so I donned rain jacket and hustled. Twice, dramatically, as I peered down for footholds on the trail, I saw flash of lightning reflected on the ground around me and in a split second thunder broke over me and brought a strange sense of exaltation and vulnerability. I pulled up to look—ominous dark heavy clouds were above and wispy white ones drifted among the trees through mountain and valley to the north. Gloomy and gray and cool for the first of July. Then down the slippery path from Fall to Valley, once landing on rear rather than feet—fourteen miles and almost 4,000 feet of elevation change behind me.

How I love these mountains and Nature's artistry and power playing over and through them. I sometimes wonder that I'm not completely overcome by it, as if I'm missing something crucial inside that prevents my bursting with ecstasy.

I walk everywhere—to work, to shower, for food, to follow my dog Ed around as he explores this landscape in his own nose-first way—and I see each time the same granite walls and surmounting domes, columns, spires, and waterfalls. I marvel and bow.

— CHAPTER 16 —

ALONG THE RIVER

I'M WORRIED ABOUT ED TODAY; he's an old dog and cannot last much longer. I decide to give him as much as he will eat along with his medications, see that he's comfortable, and then make another foray along the Merced River toward Vernal and Nevada Falls, but with him on my mind. Water, as usual, soothes. As I walked, the sun rose over the Valley rim just southeast of Half Dome. Tall trees stood above the rim, backlit. One directly between my line of sight and the sun became solid gleaming white, those just to its sides had branches aglow, and the next ones out had whitened needles. Large birds, probably ravens, flying into or past the trees were unknowingly whitewashed as well.

Flesh became light. Matter turned to energy. The physics of this are straightforward but that doesn't detract at all from the magical feel of it. How variously we can experience common things just by shifting the light or the angle. There is a hiddenness to them, and when we're fortunate and attentive it partially reveals itself.

My first memory of this phenomenon comes from years ago hiking a shallow valley in the Mojave Desert, slopes covered in cholla cactus. I looked up eastward toward the rising sun and suddenly thousands upon thousands of cactus spines were deeply illuminated, glowing. It astonished me. In both experiences light penetrates and fills, whether pine needle or cholla spine. It's another way that Nature speaks. I wish I were more articulate about this. I listen and something out there moves me.

Walking down from Nevada Fall on the John Muir Trail, I come to an area where the trail descends with high granite wall rising almost vertically to one side and steep falling slope on the other. Snow-melt flows gently down the wall. A narrow lip transects the wall fifteen feet above me and drinking-straw-sized waterfalls arc out, descend a few feet through the air, strike granite, and shatter into bursts of droplets that spread gaily out, some in free fall and others back onto the wall. These too captured the sun and shone diamond-like. Even more enchanting, the granite wall had a multitude of tiny garden spots all the way down, anywhere there was moisture to nourish them. A slit here where purchase could be got, an indentation there, cracks, wrinkles, creases, and often moss and lichen had gathered sufficiently to lay down a welcoming bed. A bit of grass, a tiny flower—these were randomly scattered over the surface and all seemed to flourish in their precarious perches. Such liveliness.

What happens in a few weeks, though, when the water dries; how long can they last? I suppose they do their work quickly—sprout, seed, spread their energies around; enjoy their floral being and allotted time; bedazzle passersby with their courage and beauty and improbability. And then pass on.

If someone asked if trees and flowers could grow out of a granite base, what would you answer? Obviously not, you'd probably say. But the Sierra Nevada proves otherwise. Look at domes high above and you see they have tree "follicles" where none would seem possible. Up close I have seen fifty-foot-high trees sprouted out of what appeared inhospitable rock. All over these granite mountainsides and mountaintops I see exuberant growth. It astonishes. Again and again, I look.

As with the physics of light, botanical and geological science can explain all this. The nature of these plants is to reproduce; birds and wind scatter seeds; water and minerals and sunlight do their jobs. I understand all that, and appreciate what it has to teach me. But I hear more, for empiricism is only one party to the conversation.

Why the exuberance, this clear determination to spread life and beauty to the four winds? Why does Nature bother? What is the point? I don't know; life has its own purposes and capacities, but as I stand before that wall, water droplets falling on my face, eyeball to a tiny leaf that homesteaded this granite wall, feeling a responsive love for that water, that rock, that sunlight and air, that adventurous, eager little plant, I do know that a lot happens on this Earth that doesn't fit our categories, and I earnestly give thanks.

There are sometimes funny little surprises on the trail. I looked down toward the Merced and saw a placard on a stand in what appeared an odd location, so I diverted and made my way down. It looked as if it had been there a long while, a quote from John Muir posted on it: "...rocky strength and permanence combined with beauty of plants frail and fine...water descending in thunder, and the same water gliding through meadows and groves in gentlest beauty." A few feet away, on another stand planted on the riverbank (amidst boulder and steep slope and trees—a lovely spot, no wonder someone chose this place to pause) was another placard: "CAUTION: Slippery rock surfaces." Someone feared that Muirian lyricism would make people careless.

At the top of Vernal Fall, a bush reaches out over the cliff and looks down 300 feet. Among the leaves and branches, foraging obliviously (and making me nervous) was one of the ubiquitous ground squirrels. After a few minutes he returned nonchalantly to rocky solidity. I want to know how he appraised the danger. Brave and agile, he may not think it worrisome.

— CHAPTER 17 —

SOUTH FORK
OF KINGS RIVER

Day One

IT IS LATE SPRING OF 2016 but rainy and cold. I'm in Kings Canyon looking up the mountainside as wisps, patches, and skeins of cloud weave among the pine and fir that stand taller than their brethren. Farther east canyon walls heighten and northward faces still harbor snow. It was an average snow year (in contrast to the last four drought years) and the River gathers and concentrates its melt and gravity carries it down and out to the west, excitedly as if fleeing or anxious to get somewhere. Soon it will water crops of fruits, nuts, and vegetables in the Central Valley, and it is altogether likely that some of it will end its journey nurturing me also as I savor the food it makes possible.

The River's about fifty yards wide and its surface a maelstrom of swells and white bubbles as it passes over and around or glances off large rocks that aren't quite boulders. It seems pure in its transparency and carries nothing on its surface but bubbles and reflections.

185

John Muir often called such streams joyous but this one seems too serious for that. Maybe later when it's not so busy, or is it just me feeling the weather's gloom, not willing to share the River's joy?

I plan to be camped here for several days and my project is to get to know this River better. I will sit and walk beside it for several hours every day, although not today in the rain. There are trails up the canyon sides and from past years I know they go places I like. They speak as they always do but I cannot accept the invitation this year. Some leg problems have conspired to make climbing painful, actually impossible for those distances, so I have learned to hike on less demanding trails. A big change after forty years of jogging and mountain hiking and a surprising one. I had foolishly counted on legs of steel to carry me into my later years more or less unchanged, but steel had other plans and appears to have gone the way of all things. Another young man's delusion has to be set aside.

I thank Marcus Aurelius, Epictetus, and other Stoic and Buddhist guides for sharing enough wisdom about the virtue of nonattachment and acceptance of *faits accomplis* that I know now to engage sitting, when I must, as I once engaged hiking and running and to learn what I can from that. But I don't claim absence of occasional nostalgia for the loss any more than when I realize that attractive young women no longer look at me as they used to even though I look at them much as I always did, one of Nature's cruel imbalances, I say to myself ruefully.

I did not choose river-watching randomly. Water enchants me, whether streaming and falling like here, ebbing and flowing like the ocean at home, or lying peacefully in pond or lake. Its versatility and resilience astonish me. The true essence of a "self" is hard to pin down but being composed of 60% water I accept that mine is wet. I don't know the why of water's enchantment and it doesn't matter, it just is. By the time I leave next week maybe I'll know more.

Day Two

Glorious sun and warmer today, a good time to find a sitting place. In this I more or less accept the counsel of meditative Buddhists and Edward Abbey, who said that the best way to get to know a place (or self, or world) was on your rump. Sit. Stay. Pay attention. I will try, but the mind wants to get in the way.

A proper sitting place takes care to find. I want sunlight because the days are still cool. A flat rock or patch of ground where legs can hang down. Close enough so the River will be companionable. Private. No sounds but River and birds. I found it within a half mile. Leisure and solitude are the best aides for contemplation and I have plenty of both, so the responsibility is mine: the River will speak, but will I hear?

It speeds past, having begun in the upper reaches of the Sierra Nevada many miles east of here. On my descent into Kings Canyon a dozen or so miles to the west I stopped and was able to look down about 1,500 feet to the South Fork's confluence with the Middle Fork. More miles west, but out of sight, the North Fork joins the gathering and afterward the trio becomes the single Kings River.

This Fork of the Kings, like the Merced, displays a powerful metaphor. Attached to the riverbed are rocks large and small. All the early tumbling that brought them here seems spent. None moves, while over and around them water rushes deliberately, shaping itself to fit. In my imagination, rock and River are aware of one another's presence; the water couldn't avoid the recognition if it wanted to since it has to swerve, rise and then fall, gather and froth a bit just to get past. The rocks are unmoved, a picture of tranquility midst the swirl of life. I want to be like that.

Early Greek and Roman philosophers of all schools aspired to *ataraxia,* an untroubled mind. Techniques varied but they aimed at the same condition. Ataraxia is an intrinsically good state, satisfying in itself (and the word a delight to my ear so I seek occasions to haul it out for use). It is also the state of mind most conducive to the best uses of reason, the achievement of understanding, seeing through falsity, and mastery of swirling emotions and external intrusions. Serene like these rocks.

I notice that Steller's Jays are plentiful and active, winging over the River back and forth often with grass or straw in their beaks. Crossing even once would be an extreme trial for me but they seem hardly to notice. Nest-building, presumably, such activities being delayed at this elevation. A woodpecker has a go at a nearby snag and then he too crosses the River. An ant crosses my hand and unthinkingly I brush him off and down the bluff on which I sit. I regret that since he'll have a long trek back up and I could have accomplished my purpose less forcefully.

The River is not deep, three to four feet at most and often less. But the rocks make a tumble of it and it's swift. Racing rivers and serene ones create different atmospheres, not surprisingly. I imagine what it would be like to be set down in the middle of this one. I wonder if

I could survive the current and the battering rocks and get back to river bank.

Several years ago I was here about this time of year after a winter of unusually heavy snowfall. The River was even more eager and impatient then but was probably a couple of feet deeper so that its course over the rocks was smoother although still choppy. I was east of here and happened to be looking upriver when around a bend I saw something coming afloat in the middle. It turned into a duck, a merganser. He rode along, rising and falling with the current, steadier than a kayak, held to the middle, took in the passing sights. Disbelief, astonishment, and finally I was all smiles and hurrahs. He seemed satisfied with himself. As he passed he turned in my direction and I'm damned if he didn't smile. He was out for the ride of his life. From beginning to end I watched him for 300 yards and it was brief owing to the River's speed. But I don't doubt that he let the River carry him for the sheer joy of it. I'd like to know where he hitched his ride and where he felt completion and rose from the current, beat well-rested wings, turned, and returned to ride another day. It will always stand as one of the most remarkable and moving sights I've had the privilege of witnessing. When I recovered I stood, bowed downriver, and whispered admiration and good wishes to my buoyant friend.

Day Three

It took a few minutes to find my sit spot this morning even though I thought I'd imprinted landmarks on leaving yesterday. I'm never as observant as I wish even though attentiveness (mindfulness) has been a self-improvement adjuration *(pay attention!)* for at least thirty years. Not a natural, evidently, and I've no doubt the deficiency has impaired my progress. It's become a joke with Lynn, who sees and remembers (not to mention smells and hears) everything and is perplexed at my occasional inertness in the presence of what's obvious to her. Even so, I may qualify as marginally enlightened, so perhaps my commitment to mindfulness as the door-opener has not been completely vacuous.

I found the spot and sat for an hour until the sun became too intense. Mergansers still like this place. Three flew downstream separately and returned as a single and a couple. This River must be their home, pathway, and playland. Every animal is admirable in his own way and familiarity reveals each species' distinctive ways. We once had a barn and meadow full of ducks, chickens, and turkeys who'd been rescued from one threatening situation or another. Most of the ducks and turkeys were domestic varieties but occasionally orphaned wild babies were introduced to the flocks. In one case a female teal joined for a couple of years and was adored by a domestic Pekin. Always together, they seemed a permanent pair, until one spring when the river bordering the meadow ran full and wild migrating ducks dropped in, and Pekin was abandoned to a desperately broken heart that did not heal, if it ever did, for weeks. (We probably could have foreseen this; the teal was always the last bird into the barn at night, often perched on top as if expecting something.) Pekin searched and mourned, searched and mourned, for days and eventually gave love another try with one of his own kind. Sans romance a similar thing happened with a wild turkey who was with us from chick to adult, at which time a wild flock ambled through one day and when it departed was one bird richer. Wildness is a great and mysterious way of life and those institutions and people who steal it from creatures who could enjoy it are guilty of a terrible wrong.

Walking the River, I step around wildflowers. Lupine and Indian paintbrush I recognize and name, but that's about it. I once made a point of identifying flowers, birds, and trees but when I realized that from season to season I forgot most of the names I gave up the effort. It was satisfying to attach names, but the pleasure of their company, the frisson of delight when out of the background steps a familiar shape and color, fellow traveler in our shared home, carries on undisturbed by the shrinking of my memory.

As I left my spot two more beauties appeared. A western tanager (some names still hang on) with color aglow, more intense than ever at this time of year. And a modest but striking flower on spindly stalk, three white petals, a touch of purple near the bottom of each, tiny yellow filaments surrounding its throat, and six anthers standing watch. I understand beauty's role in reproduction but surely this flower and tanager overdo it. Why so much? Muir was shocked into awareness that beauty serves Nature's purposes and not humans' when he encountered an orchid as he trudged through wilderness swamp in Canada. (He had absconded during the Civil War, feeling as an immigrant and peaceful man that he had no taste for a battlefield, a sentiment I joined him in 110 years later as a matter of conscience when invited to participate in the Vietnam War.) Beauty has its own story quite apart from us although we are sometimes summoned to witness and learn from its reality.

I notice that River sound is continuous and invariant.

Without straining for comparisons, it reminds me of no other sound. (Bird book efforts to convey in letters and words bird calls usually don't work for me so it might be my lack rather than the River's in failing to identify a similar sound.) It has an element of symphony hall applause at its point of diminishing or freeway traffic from a half mile's distance. It could be a source for white noise given its constancy. I listen with eyes closed and then opened, and I realize that in context it is just right and completes the River's rushing presentation. Hundreds of millions of years ago water music may have been most of the sound available.

I return the long way going farther downriver, across a bridge, and back to camp. There are times when it makes sense to speak of a river's moods, but not today with this one. Too busy for moods but it does present itself differently depending on slope, the number and size of large rocks, depth and width. I enjoy the changes and can see how the choice of a sit spot can affect the experience, as similar choices do for other experiences.

Onward, and after a couple of miles I hear a new and familiar sound. A stream comes down from the south side of the Canyon aiming to add its humble gift to the South Fork. Alone it wouldn't amount to much but consider how many of these there are in the River's watershed. Cold, its former life as snow not far behind. The River moves me, sometimes deeply, but these little side streams have their own voice and can be more companionable, more intimate. I give it a sit, too, for a while.

Day Four

Well, that was embarrassing. I spend this time on the River for several reasons, one being the hope of strengthening my capacity for contemplative attentiveness. I want to be more aware, observant, mindful, to see things as they are...and I walked right by the turn-off to my sit spot. A quarter mile into my error (mind-fucked rather than mindful, as certain human-potential teachers used to say), I began to suspect my error, another quarter and I knew. Backtrack and sure enough: It's right where I left it yesterday. I may be hopeless.

As I said earlier, climbing is painful now, so I restrict my hikes to mostly level ground. This is my first time back in the Sierra when the limitation's become so undeniable that I've chosen to accept it and put my time into other areas that matter. Every year I take 3-4 months to camp and hike alone in the Sierra Nevada and desert. I won't stop that annual custom but my participation will change. Knowing how this River engaged me several years ago I determined to spend some of my hiking time sitting, watching it flow, observing what goes on around it, practicing contemplation, silence, slowing...in a word, tranquility. I've felt myself subsiding into these but old habits, the wandering mind especially, hang on.

Today the River seems to have risen some; these warm days may be pushing snow to give it up, take a last look around, melt, and either soak in, evaporate, or flow down and away. No mergansers fly or float by; not many birds of any kind. Nor an abundance of butterflies, but several species are among those present. I discover a new pleasure: hard as it is to get up, I've taken to dropping to knees and peering into flowers large and small and respectfully spying on the beetles and their fellows as they slowly prowl blossoms. They are hardly noticeable from on high but surprise me with their ubiquity when joined at their own level. Stately, methodical, unhurried, patient with the big eye staring; they really are charming. In what I take as a gesture of community, when I sit later I find a lady bug hiking a pant leg, pausing, stretching her wings, resuming her journey. She's welcome to stay aboard as long as she likes.

Across the River a pink-clothed trio has appeared; it looks like mother, a four or five-year-old daughter, and perhaps an aunt. They walk to the bank and I think I know what's going to happen next before they do. The girl picks up a stone and flings it into the River. She is followed by mother and in turn by her aunt as well. A compulsion, particularly among children, but adults are also vulnerable. I've wondered why and now I sense an explanation. Flung stones disappear forever; even the common skipping across placid surfaces, one, two, three times, only delays the disappearance. Utterly gone. An unconscious metaphor for time and impermanence, or one's life course? Universal rock-flinging across watery surfaces seems like more than mere pastime.

I'm a little restless today, maybe foretold by missing the cut-off. So I try another spot upriver. Narrower, so the surface is a total jumble of froth, standing waves, troughs, and splatter. It reminds me that it was just this that so pulled me in at that first visit. My primary river attachment has always been the Merced flowing through Yosemite; I've seen it quiescent at summer's end and at flood stage in spring. But never have I seen it so turbulent as this South Fork of the Kings can be. But that could be mere artifact of memory. By nature I lean toward tranquility, but who could resist such vigor. Bank to bank it roils.

I take in the River with eyes closed and then open, hearing, seeing, opening to what comes. At a Zen retreat once we sat for hours meditating before a blank wall. Not my cup of tea. But what's the difference? In both you seek calming of mind, focused attention, a different consciousness. A confirmed meditator might consider a river distracting, too much sensory input. But the wall left me dull and wondering how much longer I had to sit there. The River works best for me, when I remember where to find my spot.

Water has both inherent and instrumental values. Sight and sound become artful and musical, a sensory pleasure. Always nurturant and usually taken for granted. We use, abuse, and waste it in a thousand ways. Can we learn from its versatility and adaptability? It knows when to bend and give way, and it can be a power beyond imagining. It changes state depending on conditions, and changes back when invited by new ones. Vitality through my mouth, death in the lungs. A spring shower, then flood. And so on. Yet its integrity, its essential watery-ness, always remains. Water and air: Nature's two most precious gifts. May I not forget.

Day Five

I leave tomorrow so this will be my last sit here by the South Fork. No changes that I notice although every day has been a little warmer than the one before. My preferred spot is in the bright sun so I've moved upstream ten yards. It's evident here in the Canyon and on mountain slopes that drought has taken a serious toll—large numbers of standing snags with dead needles and leaves still attached. It is impossible not to worry about the forests and the resident wildlife as climate change turns so much of the West in a desert direction. I imagine the Sierra Nevada scoured by fire, drought, and heat and I grieve. Robert McFarlane cited someone who faced his own wild losses at human hands, saying that sometimes he felt like "a man who is appalled to belong to his own species."

When I'm not sitting, writing, or walking, I spend time reading the ancient Romans and Greeks and recently a history of moral thought going back almost three millennia. The persistent question (why can't we answer it?) asks what kind of creature is *Homo sapiens?* What is his nature and better possibilities? I am satisfied to say that we were ambiguously conceived (evolutionary misstep, or as someone said of our kind of intelligence, a "lethal mutation"?), deeply flawed and fragile, and prone to short-sighted error in our choice of ends. Our better possibilities submerge too often in our inferior ones, the unreal shoulders out the real. I think it's virtually guaranteed over the next few generations that we will self-extinguish most of humanity through nuclear weapons' use and/or climate change and turn Earth into a ravaged place that in its great resourcefulness will patiently set about recovering as it did in the deep past after similar disasters. A few million years is all it will take—how I'd love to have a sit spot to watch that happen. Wise Nature's evolution will probably take a different path with primates than it did with the present disastrous version.

I am not here to lament or castigate. As I've accepted the changes that aging brings, I try to accept the far greater losses to existence brought by human destructiveness. Acceptance means to withdraw attachment and emotional energy related to occurrences inexorable, but it does not mean approving or liking them. It is not indifference. As a finite creature, I want to focus my concerns on the good that I can do and the good that I can stand (or sit) in the presence of. Like this River.

Before I die I hope to arrive at the fully experienced realization that this world was enough, that being, just being, was enough. Other than helping clean up human made messes, I did not need to "improve" it. It was here, it allowed me in, it was complete in all the vital particulars. The best I could do was to love it, and I have done that. Everything that mattered came as a gift and my return on that was never sufficient. I am grateful to have been here and for whatever time I have left.

My thoughts often go back to that merganser scudding along the racing river and sometimes I look upstream as if expecting him to return. Nostalgia probably does not receive the appreciation it deserves. It's a way to honor memory and history, and while one should not move in, it's a good place to visit. Regret does not belong there; there are other ways to pay its dues. But the times and events that were pleasing, the people who were loved or inspiring, occasions of doing good and helping others, times when I snapped to reverent awareness of where I was and that I am—nostalgia remembers, savors, probes. The future is only an imaging, but the past is still rightfully present. How else can we shape the last chapter toward what's good if we do not take into account what honest nostalgia has to tell us?

My mind wanders but I am still sitting by the River. I feel its indifference but its companionable presence nonetheless. The spots where I've sat are roughed up but will soon heal and forget. I think that what I said earlier about the enough-ness of being may have been a gentle self-admonition, for I still find myself casting around in my consciousness as if still looking for something more. Not in addition to forthright being exactly. More like something still hidden, but sensed and waiting for revelation. Probably a misbegotten yearning for nirvana, for a more confident sense of having done the best I am capable of in seeing and following the path. And in this, a little egoism I must let go.

Time to return to camp. As I stand the muscles are tight and creaky and require a few limping steps to work right. Facetiously I ask, Am I old yet? A silly serious question. I'm seventy, but Lynn refuses to think of me as old. I suspect her threshold will rise until I die. White-haired and noticing how frequently I am Sir'ed these days, the evidence is accumulating. Yet I imagine that I see the same face (nearly) in the mirror that I saw forty years ago, and when in the presence of people my age I feel younger than they in spirit and am sure they look older than me. Maybe I'm an in-betweener and will soon know the answer to my question. Will it come without illness or disability to announce it?

Fortunately I have never dreaded aging or even dying. It has felt like life improved with passing years. Still does, though I have work still in reconciling to my new hiking deficiencies. Every old guy from Cicero and Seneca to more recent writers who talk about aging enumerate its benefits. Now it's my turn.

Careers behind us, there's no more striving to get the job done, increase skills, or get ahead. We should know by now who we are and what reality is like and be living in congruence, in authenticity, with that knowledge. Freedom from schedules and to go and do, or not go and do, at will.

Companionship becomes more relaxed and "purposeless" (I include this even though I am so solitary, and happily so, that it lacks cogency). Without schedules, time works differently. It moves more slowly and deliberately, and one hopes consciously, as does the old person in movement and desire. Time to reflect, reminisce, finish answering the big questions.

Sexual desires are less intense and more manageable, ordinarily, but I confess ambivalence about this. Nature's joke, it appears, is that old ones like me still lust after desirable younger ones and even other old ones. When the occasional genital twitch disappears, I will be definitively old, or perhaps dead.

Authenticity: with senescence if one has earlier been afflicted with the "who I seem to be" vs. "who I want to be" conundrum, it's time to put that to bed. Seeming and wanting ought by now to have settled on an acceptable resolution. If not, keep trying but maybe don't take it so seriously since you obviously didn't earlier.

At peace: by now we should know that most of what agitates people is unimportant. Such aspirations as we still have are qualitative and within reach. If not, let them go. Peace and tranquility: a blessed state.

Marriage: the rough spots have been sanded down without, one hopes, the other's once beguiling uniqueness going with them.

It is time to begin stopping the **medical tests and seeing doctors,** except selectively or in extremis (no point in suffering needless pain or easily resolvable ailments). Aging should be more a philosophical than medical condition. Enjoy your pleasures (prudently): What have you got to lose?

Authenticity, again: we should be well on our way to answering the big questions. If not, get started. Time is short and they are important to rounding out and completing our existence. With these might come a sense of the spiritual dimension and gratitude.

Last but not least, it is time to think about **dying.** You may avoid the thinking but not the event. It will be the last big thing you do and you want to do it right. I started thinking about it in my thirties and have never quite stopped. (Lynn thinks it morbid but it's really not.) Among its myriad benefits, holding death within your attention can prevent your doing a variety of silly things as if you were going to live forever. The integrity of your life should be matched by the integrity of your death.

I had no notion at the beginning that this would be such a long list. There are no sour grapes here. It's a good list. I cannot help noticing that these thoughts erupted at riverside, which of course is as good a metaphor for time's passage as there is. Time is real and, as oldsters discover, brief. It just keeps flowing and will do so when I'm no longer here to take note of it.

CHAPTER 18

COSMOS

WE ARE ALL OCCASIONALLY MOVED to consider how this Universe came to be, its extent and purpose, and what our place is or should be. One prominent theme of religions aims at this speculation, often with help from supposed revelation, and with the added element of pondering God's role. For one not to attend to these questions would be like waking in an unknown place and lacking curiosity about the lay of the land and its inhabitants and how and why you got there.

Last night by the campfire the questions once again asked themselves and out of the embers came what felt a little clarifying. Not definitive, since that's not possible, but sufficiently plausible for me to accept the surmises as good enough for now. Per usual my answer began with a creation story, a short one as it turned out: there was no creation. If the choices are two—either creation from nothing or existence without beginning or ending—I choose the second. Either possibility obviously strains the imagination: how could either be true? But what's the alternative? To be more specific, I don't ask why there is something rather than nothing. I ask how. The answer—it just is and has always been; an existing Cosmos is the base condition. It is reality, there is no knowable (by us) why or how. Even so, I feel a little progress in understanding it as having been forever as opposed to the *ex nihilo* proposition. And for those with an attachment to a God concept, I propose that creative Cosmos is God and leave it at that.

Even without why or how, having comfortably set them aside, I still wonder what Cosmos is up to. A dynamic place, something is always going on, quantum leaping to intergalactic expansion. Considering the time and space scale and the pervasive, ineluctable mystery sown into the fabric, I doubt the question will find a satisfying answer or even one moderately complete. Overwhelming fascination will have to do when it comes to vastness.

We can narrow the field of inquiry, however. "Our" Universe may equal Cosmos or it may be just one of many universes. Who knows, but as presently unknowable I set that aside along with why and how. We know quite a lot about our Universe, it seems to me, although as compared to what we don't know it may not amount to much. Regardless, we have reliable information that it erupted from a tiny point into unfathomable expansion and after nine and a quarter billion years allowed our solar system to take shape, and a few hundred million years into that microbial life hitched a ride on Earth and was alone and in charge for another couple billion years, and then life forms expanded and elaborated, the atmosphere oxygenated and the oceans cooled and in fits and starts, massive interruptions now and then, Earth eventually came to resemble the place I now live. A succinct history but, my gosh, how astonishing and perhaps improbable and accidental. And this is just our small corner. Who knows what life may have been doing in others?

What is it up to with all this? What can careful description tell us? Universal patience stands out as a chief characteristic. Biological evolution appeared (here) rather late in the process and then took its time getting to what we are now, the time that most interests us. Presumably that's just how long Universe needed to get here. It was worth the wait, for it's a glorious Earth, or was until evolution tried out the human experiment. For those who like to think *Homo sapiens* was the main point of the whole thing, it may be time to reexamine your assumptions. Universe appears to be about greater things. Nearly fourteen billion years of expansion and still going—who knows why?—billions of galaxies, trillions of stars and planets, undoubtedly life spread amongst them. What really do humans amount to? Potentially great goodness and new forms of creativity, but honestly, all things considered, on balance, the good that we do stands in the shadow of the mediocre and bad.

That is obvious, and not my point. For those with ears to hear and eyes to see and sensibilities to engage with present reality, who cannot feel grateful and curiously seek truth? Whatever the why and how, it is a good Cosmos as a whole. Grand beyond words and there for the experience.

— CHAPTER 19 —

Nature Speaks

THE NATURAL WORLD HAS BEEN the place of my most reliable and deepest satisfactions. I had no preparation for this. Family, as I grew up, did not encourage it, nor did subsequent experience until I was close to forty years old. And then it was almost accidental.

My fondest early memory is of a place on a lake in Wisconsin owned by an uncle. We visited there when I was a child in the '40s and '50s. An old house without indoor plumbing; a bear rug in the sleeping attic; surrounding forest; a lovely lake with few people around—I had no distinct awareness of Nature's voice, but the place was important to me and the feel and image of it stuck inside.

A time came in the 1980s when there were funds available and I felt drawn to a lake and forest area in East Texas, a resurrection of the childhood experience. This became the womb from which my Nature consciousness was birthed along with new spiritual sensibilities. I have little recollection of what my larger aspirations were before then. I had them, surely, but don't quite remember what they were, aside from professional goals. Since then, though, my compass has always pointed in the one direction.

As Nature is where such awakening that I know occurs, it's worth digging into. I sometimes ask, "Why Nature?" and "Why particular locales rather than others?" When working on my dissertation exploring Thou-relation with Nature, I wondered about the power of the Sierra Nevada and if one shouldn't be equally affected by other places, even all places. The answer came that not only all places but all that we encounter can be a medium of enlightenment. Blake got it right in his oft cited verse: "To see a World in a Grain of Sand / And a Heaven in a Wild Flower / Hold Infinity in the palm of your hand / And Eternity in an hour." The intuition compels, and occasional experience confirms, but it resists explanation.

Morbidly, it sometimes occurs to me that the best evidence we have for some degree of free will may be the messes we have made. Any species acting purely in accord with its nature and good judgment would surely not do as we have done. It requires a high degree of misguided intention to make war on each other and on Earth as we persistently do.

I mention this by way of contrast with what one finds in the natural world. Amalgam of competition and cooperation and trending toward rich diversity and manifold sensory satisfactions, it comforts and inspires me to be there. Things fit together as they seemingly should, and even after the rearrangements and disruptions imposed by geologic and meteorological forces, they reassemble and right themselves. It feels almost as if a guiding hand were at work—not the God of monotheism but something subtler, something that inheres within and between every wave and every particle. Nature complies and harmonizes; *Homo sapiens* in its recent evolution decided it knew a better way.

It's the sense of fundamental rightness, of truth and beauty, that do it. I feel humble in their presence, but accepted and at home, even at those times of anxiety when I know that the terms of the place, its aridity for instance, or its fanged and clawed creatures, make for limitations on my habitation. And the more I'm drawn in, the deeper it goes and the closer to Reality I feel.

IV: EXEMPLARY LIVES

CHAPTER 20

LIVING IN ACCORD
WITH NATURE: THE HUBBARDS

THE STORIES THAT LIE AHEAD have led me to consider more concretely what it might mean to live in accord with Nature, in both the cosmic, divine sense of the ancient Stoics and in the more modern natural world sense, and what practical reverence looks like in these terms. I don't doubt that such lives take many forms—variety woven around a common frame, and each will surely be lived meaningfully, shaped around commitments to meaningful endeavors.

To paraphrase the philosopher Susan Wolf, meaningful life implies engagement with activities and goals that are independently worthy, that aim at things greater than yourself, are chosen out of love, and are inherently satisfying. In the Stoic way of thinking, this understanding implies a world that itself is meaning-filled from inception. One who lives in accordance seeks to fit with worldly meanings in an individualized way; we are built to make or find meaning, which emerges from positive engagements with positive aspirations and endeavors that take shape around one's most valued characteristics as an individual.

I know people who live like this. A woman who is a professional photographer and former nurse, at all times compassionate in the extreme and spiritually alert. A man who is a nonprofessional philosopher who has spent his long lifetime working toward justice for animals, people, Nature; he also is notably compassionate, gentle, and a loyal friend. Others whose names are recognizable are also exemplary. Certainly Thoreau and Muir, men who found in Nature their polestar and who lived within it deeply and reflectively. And Marcus Aurelius, the second century Roman emperor and Stoic who is best known through his *Meditations.* Each of these five are well aware of human moral frailty and each nonetheless feels (or felt) reverence toward the world and care for those with whom they share it. Strong and honorable character distinguishes each.

As I think about these ideas and people, I am brought back to a man and a woman, Harlan and Anna Hubbard, now dead for a little over a quarter century whom I became acquainted with through Harlan's small, journal-like book, *Payne Hollow: Life on the Fringe of Society.* I first read it fifteen years ago, returned a couple of times over the years, and this week read it again. I may be extra-sensitized through preoccupation with my writing, but I have been a little surprised at how these people and their lives still affect me. As I return to *Payne Hollow* I spontaneously respond with a stilled and quieted mind, a sense of being in the presence of extraordinary lives. They were neither mystics nor saints, but I find myself attributing something very like holiness to the way they lived. Not in a divine sense but as the veneration they exhibited before a physical world that appeared deeply and indubitably good to them. They lived in harmony with that. Exemplary lives in accordance with the Earth and its gifts.

As I think of them, it helps to remember what I referred to earlier as *mindful engagement,* which seems to me crucial to adequately apprehend reality. We recognize what's out there and feel its gravity. The road to truth and goodness must be traveled attentively (the road in fact is part of that truth and goodness). Harlan and Anna knew this better than most, and with no apparent self-consciousness and with rare integrity, they shaped lives together that were unique and admirable and that fully engaged them with worldly detail.

Harlan might have been described as something of a misfit. He took care of his widowed mother until her death when he was 43; he worked as a laborer and spent the rest of his time sketching and painting pictures, reading, prowling rivers, learning to play the violin, and thinking. Like Thoreau, whom he admired, he felt no attraction to what society offered in the way of conventional living. He dreamed of more, but inchoately.

Anna, two years younger than Harlan, was an honors college graduate, teacher, and fine arts librarian as well as skilled pianist. They met, came to love each other, and laborer and librarian married, each for the first time, both in their early forties. His mother died a few months later. Apparently their relationship was an epiphany for both. They immediately began to build a shantyboat and for the next six years lived on it and the water, floating down the Ohio River to the Mississippi and New Orleans, where they spent time in the bayou country. Afterwards they sold the boat and regretfully bought a used automobile (with which they never appeared to make peace since it was a machine), built a trailer house of sorts to pull behind and took a year exploring the west. Then back to the Ohio River and eventually Payne Hollow, seven wasted acres isolated on the River on which they proceeded to build a home and a life that lasted for another thirty plus years until they were in their eighties.

These were not normal people. After they married they never held a job again, living self-sufficiently and on the few dollars brought in by the house he'd built his mother, which they rented out following her death. Consider life at a place like Payne Hollow where you've built your home with your own hands, a few purchased materials, and a lot of found items (such as driftwood). You also build the furniture, feed yourself from your garden along with fish from the river and the goatherd which lives in the stable you built. Heat and cook with wood you chop and then wheelbarrow down the hillside, wash clothes in tubs, and make just about anything you need from "junk" or a few purchases from across the River. And you also paint, write, play piano-violin duets, read to one another, and are kind to neighbors and strangers who are attracted to your strange household. Although friendly, you value most your solitude and the satisfactions of living by your own hands. Together you have mastered all the skills needed to survive: gardening and cooking, raising and killing an occasional goat, fishing, carpentry, sewing, plumbing, construction, converting salvage into use...you can make and fix anything you need and rarely require bought materials. And you are joyfully absorbed in the work, even when it includes chopping and fetching firewood from up the hill in the snow.

Harlan and Anna were people for whom the word authenticity was made. Their homemade home was described by visitors as simple but elegant, even refined, and always completely neat and clean. When I consider what's involved in meaningful lives I think of respect for Nature, mastery of useful work, love, intellectual and/ or artistic engagement, integrity. I would usually include social responsibility as well but solitary lives so exemplary of all the rest, as the Hubbards' were, would not invite that, and they were certainly not irresponsible in any way. Further, the attentiveness I mentioned above seems to have been endemic to whatever they were doing. Keeping house, bird calls noticed while chopping wood, awareness of seasonal and daily river changes while repairing the boat or fishing, the rhythm of the seasons, managing gardens with year-round growth and dozens of vegetable varieties with different needs, and on and on. Such mindfulness of course had pragmatic value but that seems to have merged with ceaseless enchantment as they recognized the big meaning within little things, the satisfactions latent in everyday endeavors and encounters.

From the pages of *Payne Hollow,* Harlan speaks for himself. On a winter night, ice floes and moonlight on the River, he remembers a summer with the same moon:

> In my mind I can see the rhythmic flashing of many fireflies against the heavy foliage. The earth is good and the changing seasons are a joy.

Reflecting on the decision to settle at Payne Hollow:

> Anna and I were attracted by the very conditions which caused it to be abandoned. We are unique among its inhabitants, not farmers, nor fishermen, nor shantyboaters in the accepted sense; yet closer to the earth than any of them, with true respect for the river and the soil, and for Payne Hollow.

Living in time:

> Days and nights there were full of wonder, even the commonest and most often repeated workings of nature acquired a deeper meaning [...] It began at daybreak with the chirping and chattering of birds close at hand and in widening circles around us. And then, what greater wonder than the rising of the sun?

> All our living is regulated by the revolving seasons. They determine what we do, what we think and talk about, what we eat, the pattern of each day. Our house adjusts to the season, opening in the summer and closing against the winter's cold. The time of our getting up in the morning [...]

> We take our gardening seriously for it is the keystone of our living here. Most of our food comes from it, and rich rewards to the spirit as well. Only a gardener can realize the satisfaction of living close to the earth, in harmony with the system of nature, of knowing how to direct the forces which cover the earth with verdure so that his cherished plot of ground will produce harvests that nourish and delight him. It is no punishment to get your living by the sweat of your brow.

On building a cistern to capture rainwater in order to have a more reliable source and not have to carry buckets-full to the house from the spring-fed creek and river:

> Sweet water to drink, pure air to breathe, naturally grown food and such delights to the soul as space, quiet, solitude and dark nights—these rewards outweigh by far the time and energy required to achieve them.

Of those I referenced above as exemplars of reverent living, none chose a way that demanded as much of them as did the Hubbards. The daily demands of their life not only did not impair their receptivity to the goodness and wonders they discerned around themselves (aspects unnoticed by others), it seems to have intensified it. The immediacy of knowing that everything depended on themselves and that in feeding and providing for them in the various ways that each mundane, necessary act did, exposed by their awareness and linked with gratitude for everything provided by the Hollow, the river...the Earth, all of this transmuted their experiences into signs of the hidden meanings enwrapped within everyday reality.

As noted above, in returning to *Payne Hollow* after several years away, I still find myself deeply moved as I contemplate their lives. Wendell Berry, essayist, novelist, poet, teacher, and farmer, a man for whom I have long felt a comparable respect for living with rare integrity, is also from Kentucky and came to know the Hubbards in the last years before their deaths in the late 1980s.

In his book, *Harlan Hubbard: Life and Work,* he describes Harlan's as an "exemplary" life, not "merely eccentric." Why? From first to last Harlan had no interest in monetary or commodity measures of value, other than to eschew them consistently. He saw " [...] the overriding irony of our present economic life: that 'growth' is inescapably shrinking us." We use up landscapes as we use up everything else for profit and passing pleasures, and our children

> [...] must either make the best of them [ruined landscapes] as Harlan and Anna did—by poverty of means, by great skill, by love—or endure them at their worst.

> [...] The paramount historical significance of the Hubbards' life is that they lived and thrived in a place in which, by the conventional assumptions of our time, all human possibilities were exhausted [...] [Payne

> Hollow] was available to the Hubbards because no one else saw any good in it [...] The example of the Hubbards' life at Payne Hollow puts that failed history into a proper perspective, and suggests a proper correction.

Ironically, during their last years, the utility industry across the river in Indiana decided that the world needed another nuclear power plant and amidst great protest proceeded to build it with its cooling towers visible from the beach at Payne Hollow. The Hubbards went on as before, quietly tending their gardens. And before completion, the nuclear project collapsed.

> The monstrous wealth and power, whose influence Harlan and Anna had renounced, finally confronted them in their own place. The industrialist's contempt for any life in any place was balanced across the river by a place and two lives joined together in love. The men of the industrial dream, who served the abstractions of technological ambition, raised their walls above the trees on the hilltop to look down upon a man and a woman who served the goodness and beauty of the earth.

It requires no Cassandra to recognize that between the continued danger of nuclear weapons and climate change, which the world shows remarkably little enthusiasm for adequately addressing, the prospects for calamity sooner or later are high. From my perspective, there are only two hopeful possibilities for avoiding chaos and maybe, finally, emerging with decency. First is the tendency of most people to respond to disasters by coming together, organizing themselves, and taking care of those who need taking care of. I sat through a hurricane thirty years ago and witnessed just such responses and much has been written about that happening in other calamitous circumstances. How well that tendency would hold over the long period necessary to surmount planet-wide catastrophes is a big question. The second ray of hope shines out from people like the Hubbards who are already, pre-disaster, living in ways that are prudent, healing, self-sufficient, and minimally consumptive. It is this factor, I believe, that Berry pointed to in his description of their possible historical significance, that their way might ultimately be a buffer against the worst and present a path out. They chose to do it alone but their model for right living can serve for intentional communities as well as for others more solitary.

But the powerful effect of the Hubbards' lives on so many of the people who came to know about them goes beyond pragmatics. I press myself to understand my own reaction better and have come to this conclusion: they knew things that most of us do not; they saw into the heart of things, understood the significance of what they saw, and chose to live in ways that were coherent and consistent with their vision. Lives turned into an art. Their way composed a mystic-like awareness of essential reality, an enlightened way. I think of all the tasks necessary to maintain a life, most of which most of us now depend on others to manage for us as we follow some specialized career. They mastered each and turned the doing of them into daily sources of joy.

At the end of the day, Anna played her piano or cello and Harland his violin or viola, when he wasn't painting or writing, or they weren't reading together. Berry says that after Harlan died they discovered what became a two thousand page typed manuscript journal along with hundreds of paintings, sketches, and drawings. He was a deeply reserved man whose cup of inspiration quietly ran over.

It is common to speak of living simpler lives, lives of simplicity. Usually this refers to living less dependent on material objects, less consumptive, simpler in means while richer in ends. The value of such lives for reducing the human impact on Nature and for clearing away distractions from higher order aspirations is altogether clear. It brings utilitarian benefits along with spiritual; existential clarity perceives that few objects are as vital as lived experiences that express the better possibilities of existence.

Living as we do in what is commonly called a "consumer culture," simplicity will be a choice made against the odds and maintained with difficulty. For the Hubbards, however, I do not think that choice was an issue. For them, it seems more like the unfolding of a flower in response to the sun, a natural expression of who they were arisen through their deep awareness of the essentials and the imperative of living in accord with the world around and within them. They would have immediately understood the old Zen saying: "How wonderful! How marvelous! / I fetch wood! I carry water!"

— CHAPTER 21 —

BEYOND SELF:
DANIEL BERRIGAN

To the extent that we take into ourselves, in knowledge and in love, the True, the Beautiful, and the Good, to that extent we achieve a kind of immortality. This is an immortality as impersonal as true knowledge. In fact, it's nothing more nor less than wisdom, that state of being that fuses together knowledge of, and love for, [being] [...] the kind of immortality that we can achieve doesn't negate our mortality. We are immortal only to the extent that we lose ourselves in the knowledge of reality, letting its sublimeness overtake us [...] ordering our own processes of thinking, desiring, and acting in accordance with the perfect proportions realized in the cosmos.
—Plato at the Googleplex

I FOUND THIS CITATION MOVING even if a little obscure. Essentially, I read it as: Love of the world leads to what is True (and love of Truth), leading to wisdom. Love of world implies a Good (a lovable) world and love of its goodness and the beauty spread around it. Love of anything lifts us out of ourselves, which amplifies love of everything. My capacity for the Good grows with my movement away from self-centeredness. As I am one with the world, I am one with its Truth, Beauty, and Goodness.

True knowledge about the whole and the parts comes with the experience of reverence. The cosmos and the Earth particle of it are infinitely good and enchanting (thus their evocation of reverence). I am fortunate to have my sojourn as a small particle on the Earth particle, and I learn that prospects for that sojourn being a meaningful one depend upon my willingness to let go of self-concerns in favor of commitments to larger concerns—truth, beauty, goodness—and even the quotidian versions of these of which I am capable.

It has seemed to me that this path implies not just awe but a kind of immersion in the awe-some, a dissipation of boundaries. Dissipation but not disappearance; they become porous to reality, revelatory of true things. And it further seems that out of this comes a compulsion to care. As long as one realizes that he is united with great *being,* he wants to protect it. Children, animals, landscapes: their well-being is my well-being.

In the wonderful *Bhagavad Gita* ("The Song of the Blessed One") from long-ago India, the myth has Arjuna, the Warrior leader of his people, ask Krishna, his personified God and charioteer, to tell him "where my duty lies [...] what must I do to arrive at the highest good?" The Song is Krishna's response, which I can paraphrase as a two-part path: the way of Understanding (through contemplation, wisdom, meditation) and the way of Action (based on devotion, selflessness, right practice). It is a Song of beautiful, mystic abstraction and like the best poetry and inspirational writing foments self-reflection and exterior awareness. I mention it now because its theme is the kind of understanding that arises out of reverential encounter with existence, one which becomes pragmatic, a way toward giving reality its due through good work, protecting, enhancing, using prudently and respectfully. This experience leads to appropriate actions that may lead back to reverence, another version of the ancient relation between the *via contemplativa* and the *via activa*. But while contemplatives and mystics may concentrate on God (the Absolute, the Ultimate, beyond conception), the reverential way knows creation itself as sacred, as godly, because it just *is* the mysterious unfolding of original mystery. The one who follows this way, participating in sacredness, identifying with it, feels a natural and dutiful care for creation/existence as it presents itself in the given moment. A poor suffering child, a homeless individual, an Earth with accelerating loss of species, poisoned, over-heated, land eroded, oceans acidified, disrupted in myriad other ways...all of this generates caring response even in the face of resigned hopelessness. One wants to fix or at least alleviate it, and must try even if there seems little chance of success because it is right to do so, the practice of right action without attachment to result.

Having made a career in nonprofit organizations—social services, mental health, animal protection—I had associates whose valuing of life (human, animal, plant) was deep and always committed to securing its welfare. As responsible beings, seeing the other's pain, they could not fail to respond. I have known individuals and organizations who embodied this love and whose fulfillment came through making the love active. Whatever sparks of the spirit remain in this failing world, many are found in their midst.

In this context, let me speak about an area of human behavior that has deeply disturbed me for the last half century. I refer to warfare, which, sitting at the top of the scale of human resort to violence, will stand in for all lesser forms of violence as well. In versions large and small, more or less deadly and destructive, our species has perpetrated conflict apparently since its beginning. I have no doubt that war will exist as long as we do. It answers to fears and anxieties, ambitions and misguided desires...human nature reaches for it oblivious or disregarding of its costs. But it varies in intensity and ubiquity; some people for a time are less susceptible or have learned that its promises are empty and its consequences vile.

In truth, over recent decades it is my own country, the U.S.A., which has been most susceptible, most drawn to its use. We seem to have become habituated, as to a drug, dependent and heedless of its moral costs to ourselves and the suffering it imposes on others. It surely represents the most profound irreverence toward life, although to fully understand its desperate reach into the national consciousness, we must recognize the variety of other ways in which this disrespect for life expresses itself that are contiguous with it. We incarcerate more people for longer periods and in crueler conditions than any other country. We continue to prosecute a "war on drugs" after 45 years of expensive failure which has wrecked millions of lives both here and in those regions abroad which have been persuaded to cooperate in our mania and without any semblance of compensating gains. Guns are embraced fetishistically, and even after the horrifying tragedy of Sandy Hook, are embraced more tightly. The country was born in native genocide and nourished by slavery. And finally, no other country has engaged in more aggression and violent conflicts over the last seventy years than ours. We have a deep need for reckoning with what we have done but, rather than that, we indulge exceptionalist nonsense and persistent self-delusion.

With all this, I speak not as a misanthrope or one who despises his country, but rather as something of an unrequited lover. I once expected of it better things, but these would have to begin with courageous and wide-spread self-awareness and little survives.

I write a couple of weeks after the death of Daniel Berrigan, 94-year-old Jesuit priest and longtime war re-sister and caretaker of reverent values. I did not know him but my direction as a young man in the 1960s facing the Vietnam War and a draft notice was inspired by his actions and those of like mind. In 1968 he and eight oth-ers ventured into a Selective Service office and removed the files of dozens of men who were about to be sent to Vietnam, carried them outside and burned them with homemade napalm. For his act of conscience he was imprisoned for eighteen months. Not long afterwards, having had my application for Conscientious Objector status rejected by the Selective Service and the courts, I was taken by bus to an army induction center where I refused to step forward for swearing in. I spent the next years, until its end, protesting that War while being pro-cessed through the draft system a second time at the end of which I once again refused.

I personalize this matter for obvious reasons, but I believe that everyone must in some manner person-alize their country's war-making predilections. As a de-mocracy (on paper and in theory if only in presently attenuated reality), the state acts in our names. Its wars are our wars, or more precisely, its wars are each of our responsibility. They represent such a great evil that that moral responsibility alone should draw everyone into taking a position. Many of us once thought that ending the military draft would make it harder to prosecute questionable wars, but now we know that it has made it easier, simultaneously creating a sense of disconnection between ourselves and our wars and toward the foreign policy establishment that promotes them and the soldiers who fight them. Make no mistake—just as the nation's history is our history, its wars are our responsibility. Neither can be denied, although the keepers of the national mythos and the ruling oligarchy work industriously to comfort our naïve consciences and put our critical capacities to sleep.

Existence as a whole and in its vast diversity is infinitely valuable, a holy mystery which we can love while never quite plumbing its depths. As we pay attention we wish to honor it, to pay it respect and give it our care. And I grieve that that is barely possible within an atmosphere suffused with the spirit of violence and readiness to make war.

The inventory of violent American incursions into other parts of the world is lengthy, but let's focus on two of the worst during my seventy years: Vietnam and the Middle East. These are worse in their lethality but similar in other respects. Neither was in any sense necessary, and both were brewed in a stew of misrepresentations cooked by the war-mongers who always dominate our foreign policy. They represent a deadly combination of fear and ambition and the delusion that we can (and should, owing to divine destiny!) dominate and control the world. In both it was clear relatively early that they were enterprises hopeless of achieving anything positive and yet we hung, and now hang, on and on refusing to accept defeat. To soothe any semblance of citizen conscience, deception is our daily bread.

Fraudulent, unnecessary, imperialist wars: for Vietnam the estimates of dead (including Cambodia and Laos) range between 1.5 million and 3.5 million with millions more injured, maimed, and driven from burnt out villages and homes, and landscapes poisoned by defoliant toxins and cratered by bombs. For the Middle East (Iraq, Afghanistan, Pakistan), 1.3 million to 2 million dead with again millions injured and maimed and driven from homes. In addition, the first Iraq War in 1991 and the subsequent dozen years of grinding sanctions (prior to the second Iraq War) are said to have caused approximately 2 million deaths. So perhaps 5-6 million, and very likely more, have died from our misbegotten aggression, and their graves are surrounded by the blood and misery of shattered survivors and refugees.

As for signs of regret, none are visible. Interestingly, as I write President Obama is about to visit Japan and will include time at Hiroshima, but we are very determined, according to news reports, that there be not a hint of apology in this. How we became a country that never apologizes, that never apparently recognizes any reason for apology about anything large, I do not know. The price paid for hypocrisy, presumably.

I do not present this chronicle of infamy to shock or enrage. That the carnage is more shameful and vicious than words can convey is beyond denial, although of course denied it is: the numbers are unmentionables and the motivation inevitably presented as lofty and reasonable while the impacts were regrettable but unavoidable. We wanted merely to protect ourselves and do good for the, as it turns out, victims. Move on. But moving on is precisely what we should not do. Facing the truths that reality tells is the first step toward knowing ourselves, which can lead to new perspectives and changed ways. I have zero expectation that Americans are a people capable of such a painful and life-altering journey. Innocence alternates with victimhood, and self-righteousness provides anodyne for any seepage in of non-illusory perception. Dominational drives preclude mutuality, compassion, and self-restraint.

My point is this: in the absence of feeling ourselves enclosed within a shared and venerable reality with other people, animals, and Nature, a sense of responsibility for the consequences of our actions or for the manner and motives of their initiation will be weak and inhibitory responses less compelling. A natural movement toward honoring and caring for the great shared whole that contains and sustains us goes missing.

There is no external enforcer for striving after the good rather than the selfish and expedient. Whatever I do, whether aimed at vice or virtue, will be founded in and regulated by certain assumptions about my nature and true needs and the reality in which they play out. Reverence points in directions that instrumentalism is barely aware of. Which brings me back to Father Berrigan.

Did Daniel Berrigan's early, devout Catholicism lead to his subsequent 60+ years' dedication to social and political justice and nonviolent activism, or did both religion and activism arise in the consciousness of a sensitive child and young man whose fundamental awareness of unified being and goodness never left him and for whom

Catholicism was a suitable context in which to live out his awareness? The latter seems to me most likely. Spirituality and love (and what is the struggle for justice if not an act of love) are rooted in communion, in the solidarity of one being (being one). Berrigan's life strikes me as exemplary of one who realized reverential existence.

In 1968, as mentioned, he and eight others burned hundreds of draft files of men being sent to Vietnam. They used homemade napalm knowing that at that very moment the bodies of Vietnamese people burned in real napalm in the name of all Americans. He wrote a poem for the occasion:

> Our apologies good friends
> for the fracture of good order the burning of paper
> instead of children the angering of the orderlies
> in the front parlor of the charnel house
> We could not so help us God do otherwise
> For we are sick at heart
> Our hearts give us no rest for thinking of the Land of
> Burning Children...
> We say: Killing is disorder
> life and gentleness and community and unselfishness
> is the only order we recognize...
> How long must the world's resources
> be raped in the service of legalized murder?
> When at what point will you say no to this war?
> We have chosen to say
> with the gift of our liberty
> if necessary our lives:
> the violence stops here
> the death stops here
> the suppression of the truth stops here
> this war stops here...

Some years later, Michael Winship shared an evening with him and others during which Berrigan spoke lines from the poet Gerald Manley Hopkins:

I say more: the just man justices;
Keeps grace: that keeps all his goings graces;
Acts in God's eye what in God's eye he is—
[...]

Berrigan was a friend of Trappist monk Thomas Merton, another exemplary life. (That these men were Catholic is accidental for my purposes.) In an interview with Chris Hedges eight years before his death, Berrigan credited Merton with a toughness rooted in "the sacramental life." "He [Merton] said you are not going to survive America unless you are faithful to your discipline and tradition." He did not believe that he and others like him could have carried on against the odds and with little evident success without the spiritual core and discipline emphasized by Merton, which was proof against despair as well: "This is the worst time of my long life [...] I have never had such meager expectations of the system. I find those expectations verified in the paucity and shallowness every day I live." America has that effect when "the just man justices" and justices and justices for a lifetime.

He noted that during the prior year (2007), Boston College gave an honorary degree to Secretary of State Condolezza Rice: "It is a portrayal of shabby lives as exemplary and to be honored." Some things don't change: Last year Ms. Rice was invited by a university to deliver its commencement address, but many students and faculty were so offended as to protest until the invitation was withdrawn. Some people saw this as intended to squelch views they did not agree with, but for reasons like Berrigan's I think they were wrong in their understanding of the protest's motivations. Such an invitation as Rice received is an honor, yet she is best known for her eight years' promotion of Bush administration

foreign policies based on fraudulent assertions advo-
cating unnecessary war along with torture and other
law-breaking, leading to millions of casualties, millions
of refugees, and deep suffering. Neither she nor her ac-
complices have been held accountable. The rules apparently are different among the mutually nonjudgmental,
amnesiac ruling class, but to their credit those students
and faculty remembered.

Daniel Berrigan's long career encompassed writing, teaching, ministering and a normal array of other
priest-work. He worked with AIDs patients and the poor,
for Black people's civil rights, for peace and justice of
many sorts. Hedges attributes his deep commitments
to a "radical interpretation of the Gospels," the choice
of a sacramental life (which may also be depicted as the
natural efflorescence of a life rooted in reverence). "The
good is to be done because it is good, not because it goes
somewhere. I believe [said Berrigan] if it is done in that
spirit it will go somewhere, but I don't know where...I
have never been seriously interested in the outcome. I
was interested in trying to do it humanly and carefully
and nonviolently and let it go." The just man justices regardless his prospects for success.

Shortly after Berrigan's death, James Carroll wrote a
short piece in the *New Yorker* reflecting on the meaning
of his life. Carroll is a former priest and present writer.
One aspect of that meaning he sees in its exemplifica-
tion of writing and protesting as kinds of sacrament, in
my words doing what one must as expression of a care
ethic rooted in reverence. From early adulthood Carroll
was inspired and guided by Berrigan's life as by no other. The final words of his article speak of Berrigan's pac-
ifism and humanity better than I can:

For many, many American Catholics, what it meant to be American and what it meant to be Catholic was radically altered by the witness of Daniel Berrigan. He and his brother, long after the war in Vietnam had ended, continued to insist that U.S. militarism, and the nuclear monstrosity underlying it, was a moral catastrophe. Their insistence lives on as a potent countercurrent to the ongoing drift toward war. And their insistence will always remain as hard evidence that the twenty-first century American conscience need not have become the frozen sea across which the war on terror sails so blithely on [...] knowing him, who did not see that the United States, at critical turns during the past fifty years, might have gone a different way? It still could. Daniel Berrigan's rage against war was fueled by his undying hope rooted in faith that peace is possible. I believe that, too. For the rest, I will never forget the man, or what he meant to me. I love him.

— CHAPTER 22 —

BEING MOUNTAIN: NAN SHEPHERD

I believe that I now understand in some small measure why the Buddhist goes on pilgrimage to a mountain […] It is a journey into Being; for as I penetrate more deeply into the mountain's life, I penetrate also into my own. For an hour I am beyond desire. It is not ecstasy, that leap out of the self that makes man like a god. I am not out of myself, but in myself. I am. To know Being, this is the final grace accorded from the mountain.
—N. Shepherd, The Living Mountain

AS I WAS BEGINNING TO revise and edit this book, I read someone else's that I had no real knowledge of and no expectation of finding more than satisfying relief from absorption with my own work. I was quite wrong about that. It was a remarkable book, and I quickly became thoroughly engaged with it. I read it once, and read it again and felt I had met someone who, were she still alive, would know exactly what I'm saying here—after all, she had lived it before I was born and continued

233

doing so as my own life was finding its way. She became my third exemplary life.

The Hubbards were first. I chose them because they exemplified what I consider a uniquely pure form in which a reverent relation with existence may manifest. They knew where they were and seemed to know why. Observant, appreciative, sensitive to the myriad gifts of creation—their lives faithfully demonstrated simplicity, skillful practices, and sufficiency of means and ends alloyed with profundity of vision and depth of engagement (not to mention an admirable marriage). If their way of living were universalized, allowing for individualized expressions, we could know that existence was in good hands.

In contrast, Daniel Berrigan lived a consecrated public life, one exemplary for its selflessness and commitment to values serving the largest good. Peace, justice, compassion—as with the Hubbards, universalize his way and know that the world is in caring hands safely preserved for the good of all. His knowing was of a deep and good reality, and this knowing inspired him to act on the everyday sacrality of everyday things, to love and protect them.

Nan Shepherd was born in 1893 in northeastern Scotland, where she lived until she died 89 years later, a woman with strong roots. She taught English for over forty years at the local college where she had gotten her degree. Except for traveling from time to time around Europe, Scandinavia, and South Africa, she remained where she had been planted by birth. And how remarkably she flowered there! Her book, *The Living Mountain*, was one of its fruits.

The Cairngorm Plateau is a smallish region adjacent

to her home village. On the map it looks to be roughly twenty miles square and consists of several peaks (up to around 4,000'), a broad plateau, and numerous valleys, lakes, and streams that drain it. Situated as it is close to sixty degrees north latitude with North Sea to the east and Atlantic to the west, it endures long severe winters with considerable snow, high winds, and fog. A great granite outcropping of ancient subterranean forces, it was once as high as the Alps but the eons have whittled it down. Shepherd's life, as much as anything, seems to have been a love affair with the Cairngorm. And the book a kind of diary of how that affair commenced, what fed and maintained it, the shape and feel and texture, and of how it became definitive of who she was. The affair was deeply physical and radically, comprehensively sensual (all 5 + 1 of her senses), an experiential transignification of matter into spirit.

The book was written during the last years of World War II and then lay silently in a drawer for thirty years before being published in 1977. I wonder if she may have felt it somehow excessive, too lavish in its words of devotion for the times or the Scottish temperament. She had published three novels and a book of poetry during the 1920s and 1930s but then not much except articles for local magazines until *The Living Mountain*. I am grateful that it survived its time in the dark drawer and is here now to offer its gifts.

Shepherd intends her short book (just over a hundred pages) to serve as explanation and description of what she felt was an extraordinary relationship between a person and a place:

> Summer on the high plateau can be delectable as honey; it can also be a roaring scourge. To those who

> love the place, both are good, since both are part of
> its essential nature. And it is to know its essential na-
> ture that I am seeking here. To know, that is, with the
> knowledge that is a process of living. [...] Something
> moves between me and it. Place and a mind may in-
> terpenetrate till the nature of both is altered. I cannot
> tell what this movement is except by recounting it.

And recounting is what she proceeded to do.

The attraction began when she was a child, but it
was maturity that moved her beyond experiencing the
Cairngorm mostly for its effects on her (the sensations:
"the startling view, the horrid pinnacle") to a place where
she began to see it as the individual that it was: "Yet often the mountain gives itself most completely when I
have no destination, when I reach nowhere in particular,
but have gone out merely to be with the mountain as
one visits a friend with no intention but to be with him."

When Shepherd speaks of "the mountain" she means
a composite of plateau, peaks, streams, other topographical features, all the plant and animal life that makes
home there or passes through, as well as its weather and
the people who live or visit there. The Cairngorms are a
changeable but consistent unity, a whole that is uniquely itself. Her primary source of knowledge is physical,
the revelations of her senses, and *Mountain* proceeds
through its dozen chapters to describe the elements of
its composite self and the interaction between them and
her sensoria: Chapter 4 is Water, 5 is Frost and Snow, 6 Air
and Light, 7-9 Life—Plants, Birds, Animals, Insects, Man.
To know the mountain she must know all of these ways
that it expresses itself. Chapter 10: Sleep tells of the perceptions that arise with the altered states surrounding
stages of sleep at different times of day and night, inside
and outside her tent.

> Well, I have discovered my mountain—its weathers,
> its airs and lights, its singing burns [streams], its
> haunted dells, its pinnacles and tarns, it birds and
> flowers, its snows, its long blue distances. Year by
> year, I have grown in familiarity with them all. But if
> the whole truth of them is to be told as I have found
> it, I too am involved. I have been the instrument of
> my own discovering; and to govern the stops of the
> instrument needs learning too. Thus the senses must
> be trained and disciplined, the eye to look, the ear
> to listen, the body must be trained to move with the
> right harmonies. I can teach my body many skills by
> which to learn the nature of the mountain. One of the
> most compelling is quiescence.

"Quiescent perceptiveness" arises around sleep and allows "[...] pure intimacy with the tangible world." "I have let go my self." "[...] just seeing, not bedeviled with thought, but living in the clear simplicity of the senses." Later she speaks of the separate realities of world and self: "And it is the fusion of these two realities that keeps life from corruption." Clearly she does not see this affair of hers in terms sometimes spoken of as "airy fairy"; it is founded in Earth as solidly as those roots that held her in place the entirety of her life.

The fusion that Shepherd speaks of consummates in Chapters 11: Senses and 12: Being. "[...] simply to look on anything, such as a mountain, with the love that penetrates to its essence, is to widen the domain of being in the vastness of non-being. Man [a person] has no other reason for his existence." The Cairngorm is rooted in Earth and infused with mystery. She recognizes that if she had more than the ordinary set of human senses, "other modes of perception," there is undoubtedly more, presently unimaginable, that she could learn about "the total mountain."

Yet, with what we have, what wealth! I add to it each time I go to the mountain [...] It is an experience that grows; undistinguished days add their part, and now and then, unpredictable and unforgettable, come the hours when heaven and earth fall away and one sees a new creation. The many details [...] come for a moment into perfect focus, and one can read at last the word that has been from the beginning.

[...] But no metaphor, *transparent,* or *light as air,* is adequate. The body is not made negligible, but paramount. Flesh is not annihilated but fulfilled. One is not bodiless, but essential body.

[...] a profound harmony, deepening into something that resembles trance, [where] I discover most nearly what it is *to be.*

I don't know if I have read anywhere a description of pure love for another person or another anything that so adequately depicts what it is to experience essential truths and to relinquish oneself into the union that they portend. The only explanation for this that makes sense to me is that early in her life, probably during childhood, she sensed/intuited/experienced that relational something, the interior shape-shifting, that can arise between one who is receptive and another. She took it seriously and committed, along with her other commitments, to responding and following it to its source and culmination.

The importance of all this? Shepherd speaks of irradiating the "common" to "make something universal" of it. The extraordinary, no more than the small, ordinary, and undistinguished, shine in the light of mindful engagement, evoke love and wonder. Philosophically and spiritually she was a more "meaning-filled" person thanks to the efforts she put into the mountain and the insights she drew from it. And beyond that?

At some point in my reflections on her mountain experiences I recalled something I discovered over 25 years
ago—it was Aldo Leopold's *A Sand County Almanac,* parts
of which must have been written while she too was writing; it was first published in 1949. He speaks of learning
"to think like a mountain." For Leopold also the mountain is a composite of all the life it hosts in addition to
its obvious features of dirt and rock. Mountain thinking is ecological thinking, a conviction that was forced
on him as he watched the dying of a wolf that he had
thoughtlessly shot. A wolf's howl is attended to by the
creatures that are part of a mountain—"Yet behind
these obvious and immediate hopes and fears there lies
a deeper meaning, known only to the mountain itself.
Only the mountain has lived long enough to listen objec-
tively to the howl of a wolf." As he watched the wolf die
he became newly aware of "[...] something known only
to her and to the mountain." Explicitly he refers only to
the ecological dynamics among deer, wolves, and plants
and of how non-mountain thinking ignores these at its
and the mountain's peril. But he must allow more than
this: "Perhaps this is behind Thoreau's dictum: In wildness is the salvation of the world. Perhaps this is the
hidden meaning in the howl of the wolf, long known
among mountains, but seldom perceived among men."

Leopold had been a forester and ecologist for many
years but along the line things shifted, and I don't doubt
that his watching "a fierce green fire dying in [the] eyes"
of that mother wolf was part of his change. He died only
weeks after finishing *Almanac* and was only in his early
sixties, but by then he was as well known for his "land
ethic" as for any of his scientific work. Thinking like a
mountain depends upon profound identification with

the mountain, one which elicits protectiveness and love, and both his writing and his restorative attention to his home place in Wisconsin reflect this relationship.

As far as I can tell Shepherd's identification with the Cairngorms remained at the level of devoted relation without going farther. Something about her being a woman living in Scotland during the time she did may have shaped it this way. In her Foreword, writing at the time of publication thirty years after writing the book she noted many changes in the mountain, mostly having to do with "development": bulldozers, chairlifts, restaurants, roads. And even in Chapter 9: Life: Man, she recognized the human impacts on the Cairngorm's plant and animal life. But there's no indication she was upset or thought the effects objectionable. Perhaps even one with her devotion was captive to the progress mythology, or maybe this: she could see the increasing human separation from Nature and she grieved its likely eventuation in physical/spiritual diminishment and so in life meaning. More than "development" and more than displaced birds and trampled flowers, it may have been this lost vibrancy, the lost excellence of lives, that concerned her. In this respect, she was more Hubbard than Berrigan.

It is possible I was drawn to read *The Living Mountain* because of its long introduction by Robert McFarlane, a writer whom I have over recent years come to appreciate. But there is a matter that both he and Shepherd address that I think they may have misunderstood. One of the key recognitions that comes from reverential I-Thou relation is that it is the *nature of the relation* rather than *that with which I relate* that is distinctive. Reverence lights up and enlivens its subjects in the mutuality of their presence to one another. Our Thou may be a human or

Nature where their intrinsic value stands clear, or it may be a worn-out, degraded, unloved Payne Hollow, which the Hubbards' love brought back to its fuller life. Shepherd is anxious that the reader not misunderstand her—her affair with the Cairngorms does not result from "witcherie," incantation, or "spells." It arose from "fusion" between her and world and no superstition helps to explain it:

> It would be merely fanciful to suppose that some spirit or emanation of the mountain had intention in thus absorbing my consciousness so as to reveal itself to a naked apprehension difficult otherwise to obtain. I do not ascribe sentience to the mountain; yet at no other moment am I sunk quite so deep into its life. I have let go my self.

Similarly, McFarlane says that,

> Shepherd knows, of course, that this is largely delusory: that granite does not think, that corries [recessed areas] do not sense our entry into 'their' space, and that rivers do not quench our thirst with pleasure or with resentment. She must not be mistaken for preaching either a superstitious animism or a lazy anthropomorphism. She offers, rather, a rigorous humanism [...]

My earlier discussion of Muir, Abbey, Krutch, and others spoke to the question of anthropomorphism and by implication of animistic types of attribution. I think it important to mention again because it seems to me a distraction, a missing of the point, to worry whether the tree, or bird, or landscape actually feels good to be alive as one may sense in the transport of identification and reverential apprehension. I suspect there's more there than we can know and that a rudimentary consciousness may be omnipresent, as some who study consciousness are beginning to suggest. But it is absolutely to the point to recognize that in this realm the relation itself is alive and consequential, Shepherd-with-mountain, simply because *I* speaks *Thou,* and in that helps make a beloved world. The love of those people, the Hubbards for Payne Hollow, Leopold for his Wisconsin farm, and Shepherd for the Cairngorms, reveals much of the truth that ordinarily lies hidden. Both land and people participate, each in their own ways, in the mutuality that forms between them. And that is enough.

V: Closing

CHAPTER 23

COMING TO TERMS
WITH THE PRESENT

I'M NEARING THE END AND want to say something more about why I wrote this book, which was chiefly for two reasons. First, because the experience of reverence and the understandings derived from it were arguably the main influence on my adult development. Not that it sprang forth *de novo* as a reversal of many or most of my previous ways. My commitments to social justice and peace (the Viet Nam War and military draft were a bracing stimulant for thinking deeply about this) showed themselves in my twenties, which had the good fortune of occurring in the 1960s when one who was susceptible to such concerns had plenty of material to work with. My career path traveled from social work through mental health therapy to animal protection, all of which show a clear inclination toward helping the hurting. But it was in my late thirties when comparable commitments to the natural world arose as I was drawn increasingly to spending time in that world.

The second motivation developed over recent years. I came to see the kinds of work I'd done were all premised on the assumption that things could be made better, both in the larger world of social and political processes and the smaller one of individual lives. I now see that this was an optimism rarely justified by present cultural circumstances, circumstances in which something crucial has gone missing from the collective soul. The culture and most of its people seem no longer able to ask pertinent questions about how we came to this turn and what's wrong and what might work better if well-being for all were our goal. A metastatic spread of materialist-consumerist psychology dominates the national psyche and appears to leave little room for unfettered reflection on the important questions. The result, it seems to me, is that people are punch-drunk from battering by the insecurities, anxieties, and insipidities of consumerist culture, one consequence of which has been replacement of qualitative aspirations by ones more quantitative, hedonistic, or survival-oriented.

Facing this has been disillusioning and saddening. I look at the American response to climate change as the perfect metaphor. Something serious is plainly in the works if we stick to our usual way of doing things—there can be no responsible doubt about this. But the implacable corporate and political forces of wealth, ideology, and self-centered duplicity purvey their dogma in such profusion that the populace tends to subside into confused semi-consciousness, and the usual ways continue with change that is too little and too slow for us to expect serious and timely remediation. The most calamitous possibilities seem to me the most likely, whether sooner or later.

I don't know how to change this and have lost hope that anyone will find a way. It isn't that appropriate responses do not exist but that people don't ask the questions and may not know any longer how to ask them or what to ask. Our species has had a two hundred thousand year or so run but looks as if its flaws have outraced its strengths and it is ready to pass on. Not with conscious awareness but via *la belle indifference* of the sort that jokes about arranging chairs on the Titanic draw upon.

Despair, however, is neither appealing nor productive. Which is why I have tried to show what a difference a reverent experience of being alive can make. Among other benefits, it awakens one from sleep-walking and you can notice the danger you were in and the beatitude of changing course. Maybe it's just old habit, but even in my radically disillusioned condition, I can't help metaphorically fingering my beads and muttering wishfully.

I don't believe it possible to experience the Earth reverentially and not be stunned by how irreverently (and comprehensively so) the ruling attitudinal, and especially economic, systems operate. To whatever limited extent people engage in reverence talk it is mostly about an otherworldly God, which is clearly not any part of my intention. A similar bias shows up when they speak of the sacredness of life but only mean *human* life. In both of these, the perspective is too limited and the words too often hollow: if reverence is only vertical and abstract (God) or horizontal and limited to a single species and equally abstract (humankind) then it fails to fully grasp reality as it can be known experientially, and it lacks ethical gravity. If one species is sacred, surely all are.

This understanding profoundly affects judgment,

which becomes robustly ethical. Recognizing the present normality of irreverent ways of relating to others (Nature, fellow humans), you may feel rage and grief at what appears implacably ecocidal and cruel. Alongside its daily run of offenses against comity and solidarity, the cultural system that valorizes power and wealth above ethics has created the means for its own and the world's destruction and steadily deceives us all about what's going on. The persistence and expansion of nuclear weapons and the prospect of nuclear annihilation? Why, that's merely deterrence and national defense; they have it all under control, trust them. Climate change? The present charade of an adequate response will give birth eventually to climate engineering and adaptation; look away, trust them some more. But who cannot recognize the unnaturalness and central moral decay permeating these views, the presently controlling views, and the ones that in all probability will bring the world to grief in one large form or another.

So we can turn away or we can adopt a clear-eyed confrontive attitude toward this that allows one to carry on with equanimity and that may even produce change. But not, I think, with much optimism. I have wondered grimly if humans even deserve to survive, considering the risks that we create and the damage we do and the evident fact that Earth and other life would be better off without us. It should be sobering that humans add little value to existence per se while taking from it in every way we wish (while adding, ironically, too little of real value to our own forms of existence, on balance). At present, it seems to me that those who share this lack of optimism confront the dilemma of building valuable lives in the midst of a failing culture and an at-risk existence.

Believing that things will get no better and probably worse, how can one achieve detachment and Stoic acceptance while retaining energy to define a relation to that reality that is still personally meaningful and open to redemptive openings if they occur?

Early Stoics believed that an inherent concern for others' well-being was implicit in the nature of existence, including humans', and that, insofar as one could make a positive difference, it was a person's responsibility to try. Reverence coheres with that belief for it too recognizes the innate interconnectedness of all beings. For anyone determined to make sense of the present existential predicament, certain factors must be included in the analysis.

Since power in the U.S. has clearly been gathered into the hands of a small political-economic class, the odds of making change through existing conventional political channels are remote. Consolidation of power by a few combines with complaisance among the many, the malleable citizenry, to create inertia and maintenance of the status quo except when exacerbating it. This suggests that endeavors to work toward a better society must include efforts to make radical democratic commitments in both the political and economic spheres. Political democracy has mythological status and most Americans are convinced that it is how we are governed, but we do not exercise democratic responsibilities effectively so democracy has become more form than substance. Research by political scientists demonstrates that Congressional votes are reliably guaranteed to follow the dictates of moneyed interests even when majorities of their constituents express opposition. Martin Gilens and Benjamin Page, for example, put it this way:

"Multivariate analysis indicates that economic elites and organized groups representing business interests have substantial independent impacts on U.S. government policy, while average citizens and mass-based interest groups have little or no independent influence." In spite of this, incumbents generally win elections, which is an excellent demonstration of citizen passivity.

Economic democracy, on the other hand, has rarely even been considered since most working people (in the U.S. at least) assume that they occupy a properly subsidiary role in the workplace, controlled by owners and bosses in whose competence and benevolence employees apparently place great faith. But a society of political and moral equals that aspires to providing for the basic welfare of all its members cannot succeed if power is held by only a few.

We must be inspired to become active agents in correcting excessive concentration of wealth and power and in maintaining effectively egalitarian systems of societal regulation. (Wealth and power have the appearance of highly addictive substances in their effects on human psyches and must be controlled by the citizen system or those addicted will do the controlling for they are relentless and seemingly unlimited in their dependency.) We should look for expansion of co-ops, credit unions, NGOs, worker owned businesses, publicly controlled industries, and effective employee participation in decision-making at all levels of other businesses. Individual dignity and moral equality suffer from authoritarian hierarchies wherever they are found.

Society and economy should exist to serve the common good of humans and Nature. Seeing human and natural worlds (not that they are essentially separate) as sacred vessels, the effects of economic and other societal choices on the moral texture of these worlds is the first measure of their acceptability—not profit, expediency, efficiency...but goodness and beauty and happiness. Building structures of solidarity, communities of humans-within-Nature, creates paths of intrinsic satisfaction and daily usefulness; it does not compromise, it supports, future goods.

At the political level, what is generally called social welfare democracy looks like the system most consistent with aspirations to live within good societies. Since human welfare depends on a healthy natural world, the rule is to do no unnecessary harm (prominently including, under present circumstances, no more harm to climatic processes). To ensure that basic needs of all are provided for, effective social democracy would assure public education, universal health care, employment with adequate recompense, adequate food and housing, responsive government, protection of freedom and privacy, public safety, respect for differences. Society has become subsidiary to economy and its ruling class. Society built for the good of all requires the reversal of this: economics as if people mattered more than wealth for a few.

Lastly, no honorable polity can pursue imperialistic aims and spend its resources on persistent violence and preparations for war. Millions have died and millions more suffered from misbegotten American fear and world domination impulses over the past half century. Reverence for life mandates that violence serve only as a truly last resort and that we promote international community when possible and international civility otherwise. Humanitarianism rather than militarism, talking rather than fighting.

One might envision the emergence of a range of small scale models of citizen engagement and cooperation. From organic farming to mutual aid collectives, the sparks of movement toward a much better society could arise. The experience of solidarity and partnership makes a powerful alternative to the fragmented, competitive ways fostered by the present system.

More concretely, alternatives guided by what? Is there a secular moral ethic that reflects a reverent sense of existence, a morality to parallel a political ethic such as social welfare democracy? I believe there is, but it must struggle through a fundamental human impediment. Iris Murdoch, the late philosopher and novelist, put it succinctly and colorfully 45 years ago:

> The problem is to accommodate inside moral philosophy, and suggest methods of dealing with the fact that so much of human conduct is moved by mechanical energy of an egocentric kind. *In the moral life the enemy is the fat relentless ego.* Moral philosophy is properly, and in the past has sometimes been the discussion of this ego and of the techniques (if any) for its defeat.

"The fat relentless ego": self-centeredness with its myriad shapes and masks subverts goodness. Just as power and wealth have a predictable anti-social momentum when allowed to, so do other egoistic desires. But a person may will to realize his "best self" and with that recognize that its realization is innately tied to his forms of relatedness to fellow humans and the natural world. Individuality best differentiates and expresses itself through these relations and the practices in each that most engage best selves.

Reverence for existence recognizes the fundamentally *real* and foments reciprocal presence to its truth and to its beauty and goodness, whose genuine worldly penetration it does not doubt. At the same time it recognizes that the Buddhist insight into the reality of suffering is accurate and that most people can, but few people will, follow this truth from diagnosis toward its mitigation in the search for wisdom and practice of compassion. Reverence does not seek utopia, for we are not up to that; rather, it creates a propensity to manifest its presence through meaningful endeavor and commitments to what is larger than the self.

Over the past few decades, feminist philosophy has described what seems to me one of the most fitting ethical expressions of a reverential attitude, what has been called an *ethic of care*. Caring for the good of relations themselves and the good of the other. My *good* is identified with their *good*: it is better for the other, the world, and myself that I care. We are social beings whose well-being includes individuality and autonomy that are embedded within caring communities. There's nothing new in this. Roman Stoic philosophers two millennia ago said it: We are born for each other. The same sentiment is expressed in Buddhist *compassion,* Christian *caritas,* Jewish *righteousness* (kindness, benevolence, humility...), Muslim *zakat* (alms-giving), versions of the *Golden Rule* present in every major religion...care is not a controversial commitment, despite its diminishment within societies dedicated mostly to economic pursuits.

Another way of saying this: In 1908, the American philosopher Josiah Royce published a series of lectures as *The Philosophy of Loyalty.* A person is loyal, he said,

> [...] when, first, he has some *cause* [commitment to values greater than himself] to which he is loyal; when, secondly, he *willingly* and *thoroughly* devotes

himself to this cause, and when, thirdly, he expresses his devotion in some *sustained and practical way,* by acting steadily in the service of his cause. [italics in original]

This cause must be rational, worthy, and no object of a false devotion. But once found, it must become your conscience, must tell you the truth about your duty, and must unify, as from without and from above, your motives, your special ideals, and your plans. You ought, I say, to find such a cause, if indeed there be any ought at all. And this is my first hint of our moral code.

Royce was a religious man and his philosophy of loyalty arose from his belief in loving communities and the virtues and duties necessary for them to flourish. But loyalty in his meaning does not at all depend on Christianity to support it. The *goods* of existence become a cause around which good lives are loyally centered.

— CHAPTER 24 —

THE VIRTUES &
REVERENCE

SOME OF THESE PAGES WERE written over 25 years ago and others more recently. The older parts represent an unconscious preliminary to the decision to frame my experience, and my sense of the way things are, as one that is fittingly expressed as *reverence* for existence. Even so, I have never been completely comfortable with the word owing to its scent of incense and stained glass. Until today, I could imagine no other term that satisfied me.

I am once again camped at about 9,000' in a glacial canyon that spills out of the Eastern Sierra Nevada, although not the same one where I was at the beginning. I'm forty miles north. I think it coincidental that I begin and end in such similar locales, but not that inspiration would occur there. As many traditional people believed, Earth and Universe are sacred, but in certain places and at certain times they announce the reality definitively. This morning I sat in a reverie focused on the northern canyon ridge. It rained yesterday and grew cold, although it is summer. It continued raining most of the night and morning light revealed fallen snow. Mountainsides were blanketed white all the way down to perhaps

500 vertical feet above camp. I was surprised and joyous. I consider snow a special gift. One that paints the world transiently pure. Then I understood: Reverence is an attitude toward being, but the experience is one of love. *Love of existence,* per se. I am only a fleck, a microcosm, of the whole which is vast and more complex than I will ever understand. I feel awe leading to love. Existence *is* as it *is,* and I am privileged to receive. Existence is not good *because* I am here. It is good *that* I am here and have been made a sentient vessel to perceive and pay my respect.

The ethical impulse arising from this expresses itself in a variety of ways. The classical virtues align as a person's soul or character. Early training and a lifetime of contingencies are background. When I practiced psychotherapy, we often spoke of "corrective emotional experiences," which referred to a client's using the therapist and the therapy as occasion to recognize and express feelings that had previously been repressed as intolerable, e.g., grief, sadness, or anger. With time, repetition and reflection, this commonly allowed clients to unblock and grow more comfortable in their emotional lives. I now think that something like this is necessary, or at least helpful, for lighting up the soul with the sense that whatever one does should comport with one's experience of the world as a good place toward which care is always the fitting response, care being the natural ally of reverence and reflexive once given voice. The following is a sample of virtues and how they reflect a reverent sense of existence.

Compassion responds to the perception of pain, injury, loss, or endangerment affecting other life. It wants to relieve the distress and repair the damage. Threatened ecosystems, animals abused or exploited, children ne-glected, hunger and poverty: compassion intervenes be-cause life matters, pain and deprivation impede realiza-tion of full lives, and shifting one's attention away betrays our responsibility to one another, the mutuality on which good lives depend.

Care obviously goes side-by-side with compassion; caretaking works to promote the good and prevent what's bad. One of its higher expressions shows in the building of communities and societies that consciously aim to ensure a foundation on which individuals are able to take responsibility for themselves under conditions where artificial, preventable impediments are mini-mized and internal resources supported.

Generosity eschews invidious and arbitrary inequal-ities of the material goods which satisfy vital needs. It recognizes *sharing* as a key ingredient of a virtuous life. A generous spirit acknowledges that most of what it prizes in itself came as gifts of good fortune and that not everyone has enjoyed such gifts.

There are four "cardinal virtues" that have been so regarded since Plato 2,400 years ago. *Justice* as the com-mitment to fairness and everyone's receiving his due consideration. Allied with mercy, it respects individuals and understands something of how they became who they are. *Temperance* as self-mastery and equanimity prepares one for the exercise of rational appraisal and action in the face of routine situations and contingent events. *Prudence* (wisdom) is the quality that looks at re-ality as it is rather than how self-centeredness and other egregious biases would have it be. *Courage* represents the strength of will to act appropriately based on what prudence reveals and justice requires.

This listing is incomplete but sufficient to the present purpose. Experiences of radical engagement with *the way things are* (and the way I ought to be) open naturally to a virtuous way of life.

As we observe the response of societies and governments to nuclear weapons and climate change, to war, suffering, and injustice, the lack of proportionate seriousness and the substitution of meager gestures and self-centered ambitions for substantial values, it is not possible for me to feel optimism that humans will avoid self-destruction and concomitantly destruction of a large part of what I love. Even so, acts of love for existence are as important now as anytime, maybe more so. Lovers, after all, have little choice other than to act lovingly. That's who they are.

CHAPTER 25

EVERYDAY REVERENCE

THE SPECIES *HOMO SAPIENS* IS unique within Earthly life, most importantly not in the flattering ways we ordinarily and vainly indulge, but in having evolved into a place of paradox: a little bit free in will but mostly not, possessor of rationality which is limited and unreliable, fleetingly aware of higher possibilities but drawn to complacency and immediate comfort, generally peaceable but easily drawn toward heinous violence, fundamentally communal but prone to egocentrism. In short, we are bound to be unpredictable, unstable and often dangerous, and while I see no remedy for this, there are ameliorations, palliatives, potentials. I have wanted this book to portray what I consider the most vital of those potentials, our capacity for opening mind and soul to reality, its truth and beauty, to experiencing the goodness of existence and so finding ourselves pausing in silent reverence and gratitude—letting them flow through and change us.

Our survival depends upon new realizations, but who will notice? This will be the only time I cite the Bible, but I recall words from Romans: "I do not understand what I do. For what I want to do I do not do, but what I hate I do. [...] For I have the desire to do what is good, but I cannot carry it out. For I do not do the good I want to do, but the evil I do not want to do—this I keep on doing." Paradoxical *Homo sapiens,* and perhaps fatally flawed, as I suspect we will learn the hard way sooner rather than later if we do not take control over the self-destruction we have built into our way of life. (Are we doomed? Do Omar Khyyam's 900 year old words predict our fate?

> The Moving Finger writes; and having writ
> Moves on: nor all thy Piety nor Wit
> Shall lure it back to cancel half a Line,
> Nor all they Tears wash out a Word of it.)

Reverence is not naive. It is not even optimistic. Our proper response to existence as a whole is to honor and revere it. But reverence and its ethic are always vulnerable to the depredations of those with different commitments. True realism requires that while we uphold the vision, we also protect it from those lacking internal inhibitions against ego striving and its destructive practices. We can be better than we are now. I don't know how much better.

Reverence for existence as a depiction of true experience is not esoteric, although both "reverence" and "existence" portend elements of ineradicable mystery that are essential to their meaning—they indicate that something not part of ordinary awareness is at hand. Still, as experience itself, reverence is readily available even if rarely availed by most people in the contemporary world. The problem is not that existence fails to offer itself for reverential experience as it commonly did to our early forebears. Instead, innate receptivity has been masked or gone underground.

The French philosopher Pierre Hadot, speaking of

Stoic and Epicurean views, observed that "[...] there was, in ancient philosophy, a sharp awareness of the infinite, incommensurable value of existence. Existing within the cosmos, in the unique reality of the cosmic event, was held to be infinitely precious." With like mind, Buddhist teacher and scholar Stephen Batchelor speaks of experiencing "the everyday sublime," and in *I and Thou,* Martin Buber encouraged us to "hallow the everyday." Each speaks from different traditions and times and yet shares a recognition that the world into which we daily awaken bears value and meaning that we fail to awaken *to.* In our craving for "[...] security, certainty, and consolation, the sublime is banished and forgotten. As a result, life is rendered opaque and flat," says Batchelor. And Hadot, still speaking of the ancients while recognizing a persistence into modernity: "[...] the paradox and scandal of the human condition: man *lives in* the world without *perceiving* the world." Each tells of existence as deep, cherishable, and knowable with the right turning of attention.

I draw upon these people for two reasons. First, to reemphasize that a world matching the deepest aspirations and needs of human nature—a world that our nature came out of and was shaped by, that was more fully apprehended long ago than today—is right before our eyes even as we only skate its surface and deplete and wreck it. A most serious "paradox and scandal" indeed, but one that the rising consciousness of *Homo sapiens* almost certainly did not fall into for the first 95% of our presence on Earth. One in no way natural, even though industrialized societies find it useful in a utilitarian way—not natural but daily reinforced by modern cultural/economistic priorities, priorities that chiefly valorize working and consuming.

Rene Descartes, the seventeenth century French mathematician and philosopher, well known for his dualistic conception of the mind-body relation, is said to have noticed that his view of animals as unfeeling machines did make it easier (and morally unproblematic) to use them in whatever ways people wanted. Similarly, existence reduced to resource and inert background, serving no good but the human belief in its own good, places no obligations beyond "wise use" on those who would plunder or abuse it.

The neglected immediacy of this deeper-than-we-know world is a crucial distortion, which creates a crucial obstacle to one's living toward *eudemonia,* the Greek word for a flourishing life. We are invited to listen and to see, but decline or fail to receive the invitation. Alexander Von Humboldt, the German naturalist and explorer during the late eighteenth and early nineteenth centuries said that "Nature every where [sic] speaks to man in a voice familiar to his soul," and the eleventh century Chinese publication *Essay on Landscape Painting* noted that "[...] wild landscapes 'nourished a man's soul.'" The soul spoken of clearly does not refer to immaterial spirit, rather to the center and essence of a person's existence.

By way of understanding the "neglected immediacy" mentioned above, I think of simple analogies. For example, consider the familiar visual puzzle in which the dark goblet stands before a light background. At first sight, it is only a goblet, but slight change of perspective shows the stem as two people's silhouettes facing one another. Or think of a cylinder whose shadow on an adjacent wall forms a rectangle, or from above shows as a circle, three dimensioned reality reduced to two. Only a goblet, only a rectangle or circle, but the eyes and mind find more upon looking more closely.

The second reason for my appeal to the voices speaking above is to delve more into my original question from the first page: How does reverence for existence make us better people living better lives than we do without reverence? Well, one might ask, what are your standards, your criteria, the components of your aspirational good life? If relationships, ethical values, understanding reality, and spiritual experience are central, then reverence shows itself as both good in itself and good for realizing these aspirations.

Reverence self-validates and those who taste its waters and continue to drink deeply do not need my explication. And those who don't drink may not be interested or will consider it a diversion. For the modern sense of purpose, it has little to offer; it won't help anyone "get ahead." Its ROI is not bankable; it has no exchange value and may even lead to diminishing interest in economic exchange.

How does reverence make life better? Let's begin with relationships; not just those with fellow humans but with Nature and any other dimension, thing, or endeavor that you experience as truly meaningful. I spoke many pages ago about gifts, and what's involved here is something similar in that existence makes relational possibilities freely available—they are offered like air and what we can do is breathe deeply and acknowledge grateful reception. The thing about gifts and about substantial relationships (those in which instrumentality, or "use" value, is secondary or absent) is that they invoke a yearning to reciprocate. I want to give back in some manner as I have received, and in this I am made whole.

Reciprocity as loyalty, engagement, love: relations gather meaning, bespeak reverence.

Sometimes, when we are fortunate, they reach an extreme. Almost half a century ago the Jesuit, William Johnston, in his study of Zen and Christian mysticism, spoke of the fruits of contemplation, the relation of quiet presence in the awareness of spirit and world: " [...] the truth intuited [in contemplation] is the fruit of faith and charity. An intense love welling up within the heart of him who believes enlightens the intelligence, which is now flooded with a new knowledge, no longer stemming from discursive reasoning. This is the true wisdom, which only love can engender." Love epitomizes relationship and not merely as feeling, but as the knowledge and practice of giving and receiving where "I" subsides in the presence of "Thou"—in the many variations on this theme that point toward fulfillment without always arriving.

So I posit as the first fruit of reverence that we are moved to more fully engage with arenas of meaning, giving and receiving: the work of art-making, respectful participation in and uses of Nature, works of care, compassion, and justice, efforts to create humane and responsible workplaces and work processes and products. In short, the attitude of reverence sees that every venue and every act is an occasion for ethical engagement, and that both self and world are shaped by the nature of that engagement.

Which brings me to the second way in which things are made better. The experience that precedes and travels within reverence is that of solidarity, a recognition of oneness, or we-ness, identification, unity...whatever word best catches the sense that one is not alone or separate; we become bound up in relations of care with everything that matters to us, and this draws us toward virtue in the old sense of that word, of moving toward excellence of mind and act. Intellectual excellence is committed to truth and reality, while ethical excellence aims at justice, compassion, and a tranquil spirit. The second fruit of reverence, entwined with the first, comes as the love of virtue and these its fruits.

The world of Rome two thousand years ago was like our own in that its political and economic leadership was infected with self-serving ambition and greed. It was also the world in which three hundred years of Hellenistic Stoicism took root and flourished, mostly through the work of Seneca, Marcus Aurelius, and Epictetus. Seneca was counselor to the emperor Nero (who eventually ordered that he kill himself, which he did), Marcus was a later emperor, Epictetus was a former slave and later teacher; each affirmed the Stoic doctrine that virtue alone was the source and completion of happy and meaningful lives. Everything else (wealth, status, power, etc.) was "indifferent" to varying degrees. I bring Stoicism and these men in only to illustrate how things have changed in terms of a view of the life worth living, and at the same time what remains accessible.

I believe this change represents a serious loss, and not only for individuals. Absence of reverence eventuates in a world threatened by climate change (and other assaults on Nature) and nuclear weapons and endless war. It foments false consciousness, fear, aggression, and the anxiety that risks existence for material prosperity and supposed security. Roman Stoicism clearly did not carry the day then and its values are barely visible now. But they didn't just disappear; they had been founded on a still available sense of the Universe as rational and "holy," a version of the *sensus deitatis* (the sense of divine presence), a place worthy of piety and reverence and, it followed, of living in accord with the sense of its ultimate value and what that asked of one in response.

Other fruits of reverence follow from the first two. You cannot arrive at reverence without coming to love existence, coming to love reality and its truths and mysteries (which is definitely not the version spoken of by Shakespeare, the "[...] tale told by an idiot, full of sound and fury, signifying nothing."). I spoke earlier of Plato's recognition that there were people who loved the truth and would not be deterred from the search for it. And and others notice that some have a fierce love of beauty which leads outward to love of justice. And the Stoics and their love of moral goodness. Further, Plato and Epictetus suggested that piety before the Cosmos could be considered a cardinal virtue. Piety as a form of reverence. For some a part of spiritual life. They bow before what exceeds them, what subsumes self as part of the whole. Reverence.

Implicit in the view of piety, or reverence, as a virtue is its expression in practical ethics and personal responsibility. As creatures who have been shaped and determined by multiple contingencies all our lives, forces beyond our control, we still feel an impulse to seek truths and meanings, to know the self beneath the passing selves, and to join that self with others in ways that help each and all to flourish. Effectiveness at these projects is always threatened and only partial. After my years of work in social services, mental health, and animal protection, I recognize limited success and continued suffering, just as when I look out on a society sunk into self-absorption, commodification, and fragmentation, where technological and material progress have been confused with true human progress. Misanthropy, nihilism, and despair are persistent temptations. But there are ways of knowing that reveal goodness at the heart of existence and potential for its realization.

There are others that, in different fashions, speak to the motivating power of realization. Michael Frede, the late scholar of ancient history, spoke of the belief "[...] that reason by itself suffices to motivate us to do something. This is an assumption which is made by Socrates, Plato, Aristotle, the Stoics, and their late followers. They all agree that reason, just as it is attracted by truth, is also attracted by, and attached to, the good and tries to attain it." A notion with impeccable provenance and worth working with. The philosopher Susan Wolf looks at the ideas of free will and reason with a modern perspective aimed at their role in people's becoming accountable, responsible beings, albeit beings lacking full autonomy ("free will") owing to the very nature—the essentially contingent nature—of human development. Responsibility, she says, describes "[...] the ability to do the right thing for the right reasons."

> [...] right Reason refers to those faculties which will, in most circumstances, lead one to form true beliefs and good values, the power to exercise right Reason may be redescribed as the power to recognize the True and the Good. The ability to act in accordance with Reason might then be redescribed as the ability to act in accordance with, and on the basis of, the True and the Good.

Modern humans cannot be sanguine about the power of reason. Not only is it misused for bad ends as often as it is used for good ends, we know that even when well intended it is subject to distraction and distortion by a host of subliminal influences and unconscious impulses. Reason clearly remains, and always will, a vital human capacity, but after it metaphorically parties it requires a designated driver for guidance and safe arrival home. I propose the reverent attitude as a good candidate for this job. Reverence is neither irrational nor antirational; rather it folds reason into experience of existence alongside mindful engagement and love for what is true and good. Reverence opens reality and draws us in.

REFERENCES

1. The Setting

Goldstein, Rebecca Newberger, *Plato at the Googleplex: Why Philosophy Won't Go Away,* Vintage Books, 2015.

Nozick, Robert, *The Examined Life: Philosophical Meditations,* Simon & Schuster, 1989.

Otto, Rudolf, *The Idea of the Holy,* Oxford University Press, Second Edition, 1958.

3. Occasions

Gifts

du Boulay, Shirley, *Beyond the Darkness: A Biography of Bede Griffiths,* O Books, 2003.

Hyde, Lewis, *The Gift: Creativity and the Artist in the Modern World,* Vintage Books, Second Edition, 2007.

Kimmerer, Robin, *Braiding Sweetgrass: Indigenous Wisdom, Scientific Knowledge, and the Teachings of Plants,* Milkweed Editions, 2013.

Human Nature

Buber, Martin, *I and Thou, Second Edition, trans. Ronald Gregor Smith,* Charles Scribner'sSons, 1958.

Rotenstreich, Nathan, "The Right and the Limitations of Buber's Dialogical Thought" from Schilpp & Friedman (ed.), *The Philosophy of Martin Buber, Open Court* (The Library of Living Philosophers), 1967.

4. On the Natchez Trace

Coates, Robert M., *The Outlaw Years: The History of the Land Pirates of the Natchez Trace,* University of Nebraska Press, 1930.

Cotterill, R.S., *The Southern Indians: The Story of the Civilized Tribes Before Removal,* University of Oklahoma Press, 1954.

Crutchfield, James A., *The Natchez Trace: A Pictorial History,* Rutledge Hill Press, 1985.

Daniels, Jonathan, *The Devil's Backbone: The Story of the Natchez Trace,* Pelican Publishing Co., 1987.

Foreman, Grant, *The Five Civilized Tribes,* University of Oklahoma Press, 1934.

Hudson, Charles, *The Southeastern Indians,* University of Tennessee Press, 1976.

Phelps, Dawson A., "The Natchez Trace: Indian Trail to Parkway," *Tennessee Historical Quarterly,* Vol. XXI, No. 3, September, 1962.

5. Mindful Engagement

Suzuki, Shunryu, *Zen Mind, Beginner's Mind,* Trudy Dixon (ed.), Weatherhill, Seventh Printing, 2004.

Thoreau, Henry David, *The Journal of Henry David Thoreau,* Torrey & Allen (ed.), Vol. II, Peregrine Smith Books, 1984.

Worster, Donald, *A Passion for Nature: The Life of John Muir,* Oxford University Press, 2008.

11. In the Beginning

Abbey, Edward, *Abbey's Road,* E.P. Dutton, 1979.

Abbey, Edward, *Beyond the Wall,* Hold, Rinehart, & Winston, 1984.

Abbey, Edward, *The Best of Edward Abbey,* Sierra Club Books, 1984.

Abbey, Edward, *Desert Solitaire: A Season in the Wilderness,* Ballantine Books, 1968.

Abbey, Edward & Hyde, Phillip, *Slickrock: The Canyon Country of Southeast Utah,* Sierra Club Books, 1971.

Alcock, John, *Sonoran Desert Spring,* The University of Chicago Press, 1985.

Austin, Mary, *The Land of Little Rain,* Penguin Books, 1988.

Engberg & Wesling (ed.), *John Muir: To Yosemite and Beyond,* The University of Utah Press, 1999.

Krutch, Joseph Wood, *The Voice of the Desert: A Naturalist's Interpretation,* Morrow Quill Paperbacks, 1955.

Krutch, Joseph Wood, *The Desert Year,* The University of Arizona Press, 1952.

Mighetto, Lisa (ed.), *Muir Among the Animals: The Wildlife Writings of John Muir,* Sierra Club Books, 1986.

Muir, John, *The Story of My Boyhood and Youth,* The University of Wisconsin Press, 1965.

Muir, John, *My First Summer in the Sierra,* Penguin Books, 1987.

Muir, John, *The Mountains of California,* Penguin Books, 1985.

Muir, John, *Stickeen,* Heyday Books, 1990.

Muir, John, *A Thousand Mile Walk to the Gulf,* Ed. & Intro. By William Frederic Bade, Houghton Mifflin Co., 1981.

Nabhan, Gary Paul, *The Desert Smells Like Rain: A Naturalist in Papago Indian Country,* North Point Press, 1987.

Schaeder, Grete, *The Hebrew Humanism of Martin Buber,* Trans. By Noah J. Jacobs, Wayne State University Press, 1973.

Turner, Frederick, *Rediscovering America: John Muir in His Time and Ours,* Sierra Club Books, 1985.

Wolfe, Linnie Marsh, *The Life of John Muir: Son of the Wilderness,* The University of Wisconsin Press, 1945.

Wolfe, Linnie Marsh (ed.), *John of the Mountains: The Unpublished Journals of John Muir,* The University of Wisconsin Press, 1979.

14. Trees

Brother Lawrence, *The Practice of the Presence of God,* Trans. By Robert Edmonson; Hal Helms (ed.), Paraclete Press, 1985.

Citation from Krishnamurti: Source unknown.

17. South Fork of Kings River

Baker, J.A., *The Peregrine,* Intro. Robert Macfarlane, New York Review Books, 1967 & 2005.

20. Living in Accord with Nature: The Hubbards

Berry, Wendell, *Harlan Hubbard, Life and Work,* The University Press of Kentucky, 1990.

Hubbard, Harlan, *Payne Hollow: Life on the Fringe of Society,* Gnomon Press, 1997.

Wolf, Susan, *Meaning in Life and Why it Matters,* Princeton University Press, 2010.

21. Beyond Self: Daniel Berrigan

Ahmed, Nafeez, "Unworthy Victims: Western Wars Have Killed Four Million Muslims Since 1990," *Middle East Eye,* 8 April, 2015.

Carroll, James, "Daniel Berrigan, My Dangerous Friend," *New Yorker,* 2 May, 2016.

Hedges, Chris, "Daniel Berrigan: Forty Years After Catonsville," *The Nation,* 20 May, 2008.

Hedges, Chris, "Bearing the Cross," *Truthdig,* 8 May, 2016.

Physicians for Social Responsibility, "Body Count: Casualty Figures After Ten Years of the 'War on Terror'," March, 2015.

Winship, Michael, "May is the Month for Protest—Daniel Berrigan Would Agree," *Truthdig,* 7 May, 2016.

22. Being Mountain: Nan Shepherd

Leopold, Aldo, *A Sand County Almanac and Sketches Here and There,* Oxford University Press, 1987.

Shepherd, Nan, *The Living Mountain,* Canongate Books, 2011.

23. Coming to Terms with the Present

Gilens, Martin & Benjamin Page, "Testing Theories of American Politics: Elites, Interest Groups, and Average Citizens," 2014.

Held, Virginia (ed.), *Justice and Care: Essential Readings in Feminist Ethics,* Westview Press, 1995.

Murdoch, Iris, *The Sovereignty of Good,* Routledge Classics, 1970.

Royce, Josiah, *The Philosophy of Loyalty,* Hardpress Publishing (originally published by The Macmillan Co.), 1908.

25. Everyday Reverence

Batchelor, Stephen, *After Buddhism: Rethinking the Dharma for a Secular Age,* Yale University Press, 2015.

Frede, Michael, *A Free Will: Origins of the Notion in Ancient Thought,* University of California Press, 2011.

Hadot, Pierre, *Philosophy as a Way of Life: Spiritual Exercises from Socrates to Foucault,* Blackwell Publishing, 1995.

Johnston, William, *The Still Point: Reflections on Zen and Christian Mysticism,* Fordham University Press, 1982.

McFarlane, Robert, *Mountains of the Mind: Adventures in Reaching the Summit,* Vintage Books, 2004.

Wolf, Susan, *Freedom within Reason,* Oxford University Press, 1990.

Wulf, Andrea, *The Invention of Nature: Alexander Von Humboldt's New World,* Vintage Books, 2016.

[Note: References that occur more than once are only listed for the chapter in which they first appear.]

42029262R00175

Made in the USA
San Bernardino, CA
07 July 2019